MATS:
The Story of the Military Air Transport Service

THE WATTS AEROSPACE LIBRARY

MATS:

The Story of the Military Air Transport Service

by Stanley M. Ulanoff

Franklin Watts, Inc.
575 Lexington Avenue, New York 22

To

Samuel H. Ulanoff

My Father

Who Served as an Army Officer

with the A.E.F. in France

during World War I

His Stories and Experiences

First Fired My Interest in Aviation

FIRST PRINTING

Library of Congress Catalog Card Number 64-20262

Printed in the United States of America

by The Moffa Press, Inc.

ACKNOWLEDGMENTS

CONSCIENCE and gratitude impel me to say that this book was not written entirely by me, but rather with the help of the thousands of men and women of the Military Air Transport Service and its World War II predecessors — the Air Transport Command and the Naval Air Transport Service.

It was inspired by the deeds of the pilots and crews who flew the "Hump," the Berlin Airlift, and many other humane and strategic airlifts. It was augmented by the exploits of the men who fly the "overwater" scheduled routes, the airmen and women of the Technical Services and Aeromedical Evacuation.

In truth, no one man could write the comprehensive story of MATS, with its vast network of globe girdling routes, its force of transport aircraft, its historic and significant part in world affairs, its technical services, and last but most certainly not least, its personnel. The latter are, in fact, my coauthors. True, I was the instrument who sat at the typewriter and assembled the facts, but in actuality MATS has written its own story.

The present volume is the result of many thousands of miles flown in a number of different types of MATS aircraft. It is the product of five years of research begun while MATS was under the command of Lt. Gen. William H. Tunner, and completed while Gen. Joe W. Kelly had the reins. It is with gratitude that I acknowledge their help.

Valuable assistance, too, was provided by Maj. Phil Winegar, Lt. Col. Stockton B. Shaw, and others of the MATS Directorate of Information at Scott Air Force Base and at EASTAF and WESTAF Headquarters. Together with Lt. Cols. Jim Sunderman, C. V. Glines, and Gene Gurney, and Alice Martin of the USAF Book Program at the Pentagon, Lt. Col. Ray Housman, Capt. Jim Sparks, and others of the Air Force's New York Information Office, they furnished quick and ready answers to my many queries. To these dedicated people, and others past and present, upon whom I called freely for help, my most sincere thanks.

Here I must also acknowledge my debt to Capt. Gerry Hickman

for his excellent work on *30 Days* which I have renamed "A Capsule History of 30 Days in the Life of a MATS Jet Transport."

The airframe manufacturers — the builders of the new, mighty C-141 Starlifter down to the old faithful C-47 "Gooney Bird" — were also here to lend a helping hand. And when they extended their arm I was quick to grab it. Particularly cooperative were the N.Y. Public Relations representatives of the major aircraft manufacturers. Alec Anderson of Lockheed, Ted Stern and Mannie Berlinrut representing Douglas, and the N.Y. personnel of Boeing and Convair furnished needed information, photos, and diagrams.

For the many very excellent photos that illustrate this volume I gratefully acknowledge the cooperation of the U.S. Air Force, who supplied the "lion's share" of them, and the airframe manufacturers who furnished the rest.

To my family, too, goes a vote of appreciation for bearing with Dad while he pecked away at the typewriter behind that locked door, and for the times he was off flying around the world on his magic carpet — or better yet — "magic MATS."

I also extend my gratitude and appreciation to the numerous MATS people at Rhein-Main in Germany; Mildenhall, England; Châteauroux, France; Lajes in the Azores; Torrejon, Spain; McGuire and Scott in the U.S.A., and at other bases around the world, whose efforts contributed to this book.

Most of all, however, go heartfelt thanks to my publisher and good friend, Franklin Watts, and to editor Dave Knight, whose patience and forbearing through the years this book was aborning borders upon sainthood.

STANLEY M. ULANOFF

Contents

MATS:
The Story of the Military Air Transport Service

INTRODUCTION

Anything, Anywhere, Anytime

. . . I have directed prompt action to increase our airlift capacity. Obtaining additional airlift mobility — and obtaining it now — will better assure the abilty of our conventional forces to respond, with discrimination and speed, to any problem at any spot on the globe at any moment's notice. In particular it will enable us to meet any deliberate effort to avoid or divert our forces by starting limited wars in widely scattered parts of the globe.

PRESIDENT JOHN F. KENNEDY
State of the Union Message
January 30, 1961

THE LATE President Kennedy's support of global airlift was a long-awaited move in the right direction. Even when he was campaigning for the presidency, the then Senator Kennedy claimed that "our ability to meet our commitments to more than 50 countries around the globe has been critically impaired by our failure to develop a jet airlift capacity."

Global airlift is a vital, effective instrument of United States foreign policy, and a necessary component of our modern weapons system and military force. In this "cold war" era, it enables our government to respond instantaneously to pressures, emergencies, and trouble wherever they might occur anywhere in the world.

A responsive, kindly arm of the traditional American goodwill and humanitarianism in the face of such natural disasters as floods, earthquakes, typhoons, and polio epidemics, the Military Air Transport Service of the U.S. Air Force has, throughout its short history of little more than a decade and a half, answered the "fire alarm" some thirty times for major reasons. In fact, on June 21, 1948, just three short weeks after the Department of Defense had dropped the wartime ATC (Air Transport Command) and NATS (Naval Air Transport Service) into the alphabet hopper and cranked out MATS, the new service was called upon to perform the greatest airlift job in history — the relief of Berlin. For fifteen months the famous Berlin Airlift delivered 2½ million tons of food and fuel. "Operation Vittles," as it was officially called, was a resounding success, and the Russians removed their blockades and restrictions on surface transportation into the beleaguered city.

But, for the men of MATS, the "cold war" years and natural disasters that followed did not leave too much time for resting on their laurels. In quick succession MATS furnished humanitarian aid to: earthquake victims in India (1950); 4,000 Moslems whom they airlifted to Mecca (1952); victims of a typhoon on Wake Island (1952); the flood-stricken population in the Netherlands (1953); polio patients in Argentina (1956); and in Japan (1960); wounded French soldiers evacuated from Dien Bien Phu, Indochina, across the Pacific and Atlantic oceans to France (1954); more than 14,000 Hungarian refugees airlifted to the United States (1956-57); typhoon victims in Japan (1959); earthquake casualties in Morocco (1960); flood victims in Brazil (1960); and to earthquake-racked Chile with 1,754,000 pounds of food, clothing, medical supplies, including helicopters and two complete Army field hospitals (1960); the airlift to the United States of 1,093 dependent wives and children of U.S. military and civilian personnel from the Panama Canal Zone during the crisis there (1964); and more.

Militarily, the MATS strategic airlift was called upon to support: the United Nations forces in the Korean War (1950-53); Suez (1956); Lebanon (1958); Formosa (1958); the Congo (1960-64); and Cuba and India (1962-63). In 1958, for "Operation Hardtack," MATS airlifted more than 14,000 tons of cargo and 13,000 personnel as well as providing 1,100 of its own technical personnel, in support of the nuclear bomb tests at Eniwetok. And that same year MATS airlifted Thor IRBM's and their equipment from the manufacturer in California to their launching sites in England.

Since the year 1957, MATS has supported our research operations in the Antarctic and at the South Pole. On the other side of the world MATS flew heavy construction equipment, builders, housing to Thule, Greenland, in 1951, saving a full year in the construction of that key base.

MATS aircraft also participate in peacetime maneuvers with the Army. During 1960, in "Operation Big Slam," they carried more than 21,000 troops and close to 11,000 tons of equipment to and from Puerto Rico in the largest peacetime airlift exercise in military history up to that time. It was later topped by "Big Lift," the massive airlift of an entire armored division from the United States to Germany in two and a half days.

It must be noted that all of these missions were accomplished *in addition to* the MATS regular scheduled airlift, supplying the Strategic Air Command, Tactical Air Command, and other Air Force commands, the Army and Navy, and our Allies all over the world; supporting the missile program from factory to user; and supplying the Atlantic Missile Range from Cape Kennedy to Ascencion Island – more than 5,000 miles down the South Atlantic; transporting the President and other VIP's; the continuous Aeromedical Evacuation program; and the MATS Technical Services.

Air transport has always been looked upon as being quick and efficient – but expensive. It was good to ship by air when speed was essential, price was no object, and the case was an emergency one with human life at stake, as for example the earthquake in Chile and the Berlin blockade. Actually, logic and logistics have shown this concept of high cost to be "all wet." In fact, airlifting drastically reduces the excessive amount of inventory and stockpiling formerly required. It also cuts down on warehousing, packaging, and handling. A typical example of this took place when the Air Force began shipping replacement J-57 jet engines, by air. Direct point-to-point shipment reduced requirements by some 2,000 engines, resulting in a saving of $337,000,000.

Similarly, in 1955, the U.S. Air Force in Europe experienced savings of half a billion dollars by conducting its service operations by air – and had a 14 per cent increase in efficiency to boot. The Navy, too, found that it could increase weapon effectiveness and efficiency by airlift, including direct deliveries to the fleet at sea. By the same token, airlifting the 200,000 soldiers that the Army moves overseas every year, at an average saving of two weeks' travel time per man as compared to rail and ship, would be the equivalent of adding 8,000 full-time soldiers to the Army. In most cases, moreover, the troops would be at their destinations in one day. This is certainly a far cry from World War II when the men spent many days in processing at the ports of embarkation and ports of debarkation, not counting the time at sea in crowded, uncomfortable quarters.

Not only does MATS save money for its "customers" — the Army, Navy, and Air Force, and other branches of the federal government — it is the only major military command that consistently returns a profit to the United States. This is an amazing fact when we consider the many billions of dollars spent on training the Strategic Air Command (SAC), the Tactical Air Command (TAC), the Air Defense Command (ADC), the Army, and the Navy. Of course, no one expects SAC to wipe out a city with its missiles or bombers in order to train and test its effectiveness. SAC can only simulate these missions and do its bombing and missile launching on bombing ranges. Nor can we deny the need for this training, for the obvious return on that investment is the security of our nation. But MATS, in the performance of its training which is also vital to the national security, actually does the job it would have to do in the event of war. It carries needed personnel, equipment, and supplies to the far corners of the earth, and brings home the sick and wounded.

MATS flies no scheduled passenger routes in continental United States — the only gap in its worldwide schedule. However, this is as it should be. The American commercial lines amply cover the United States proper, while the MATS mission is a global one — over the oceans and worldwide in scope. So, within the United States, MATS flies regular routes only for the air evacuation of hospital patients, functions which the airlines do not normally perform. In fact, they are more than pleased when MATS airlifts a civilian polio patient in an iron lung, something that they might otherwise have been requested to do. And, of course, the airlines are not geared to handle such outsize cargo as missiles and other heavy military equipment.

In the event of a national emergency, MATS does contract with U.S. civil air carriers for a "packaged" reserve airlift of more than 300 four-engine aircraft. This is the Civil Reserve Air Fleet, more commonly known as CRAF. The drawback in this arrangement is that MATS aircraft are triple-threat — capable of carrying cargo and passengers, and capable of being converted for air evacuation of sick and wounded. Some commercial aircraft have limitations in range and are not suitable for outsize cargo nor are equipped for air evacuation.

In the words of Lt. Gen. William Tunner, its former commander, "MATS is the two bands of traffic over the Atlantic and the Pacific." But in truth, it is more than that. MATS is not only our nation's global airlift force, its technical services also provide weather information to the Army and Air Force; furnish a fast-acting worldwide rescue service; do the mapping and photography for the USAF; and until the beginning of June, 1961, provided the Air Force with a global communications system. Americans can rest assured that MATS aircraft, at the drop of a hat, will fly medicine, doctors, food, coal, missiles, aircraft, troops, or what have you, to any troubled spot in the world. Strangely enough, MATS also has had the unique distinction of having under its command the 57th Fighter Interceptor Squadron of the Iceland Defense Force.

Despite all of this flying, MATS' safety record has traditionally remained high compared with other major flying commands of the Air Force. This safety record also bears favorable comparison with the commercial airlines.

The pages that follow tell the dramatic story of the Military Air Transport Service — a global airlift force in being, traveling the routes it would on any D-day, ready and able to reshuffle and redeploy its aircraft in any emergency — a global team living up to the motto of delivering "anything, anywhere, anytime." Here is MATS' background and history and day-to-day operations; its varied services (weather, rescue, mapping, and photography) ; and its place in the world today. It is the story of a dedicated group of flying men, with a proud and hectic history, who, with the coming of their long-awaited jets, feel in all modesty that they are only now becoming a true global airlift force.

CHAPTER ONE

Flying the Hump— Birth of Global Airlift

MATS' PREDECESSORS, the ATC (Air Transport Command) and NATS (Naval Air Transport Service), were born of necessity when the United States entered World War II. In December, 1941, the Army Air Corps Ferrying Command, which shortly became the ATC, had only eleven crudely converted B-24 Consolidated Liberator bombers, some eleven Boeing Clippers and Martin Flying Boats which the Air Corps had purchased from Pan American Airlines, and five TWA Boeing Stratoliners.

From this humble beginning the ATC grew to the point where it was able to schedule twenty-six daily flights each way across the Atlantic Ocean and thirty-eight over the Pacific — as well as numerous flights from India to China, and back — over the "Hump."

From a few men, it grew to a force of a quarter of a million with 3,000 cargo aircraft. And, like "Topsy," it grew more by happenstance than by design. By VE-day ATC routes covered the world, touched every continent, and virtually spanned every sea and ocean. And this did not include the NATS' 70,000 miles of routes serviced by over 430 naval transport aircraft.

One of the most dramatic accomplishments of the ATC was flying the "Hump" — the high Himalaya mountain range between China and India. This was a case of "the difficult we do today, the impossible — tomorrow." But in ATC's case, it did the impossible "today"!

In December of 1942, after the Japanese had cut off the Burma Road, the Air Transport Command took over the responsibility of supplying China from India. Although a number of their aircraft and supplies had been "pirated" by other unsympathetic commands, they still had a job to do. The goal of the ATC's India-China Wing was to deliver 2,500 tons during the month of February and to double that tonnage shortly thereafter. The ATC succeeded in making their quotas and, near the end of the war in July, 1945, were able to deliver the amazing total of more than 71,000 tons of cargo to China for that month.

This they did by flying the 520 miles directly from the broiling sun of Assam, India, over steaming, fetid jungles infested with unfriendly headhunting tribes; wild animals, snakes, and insects; poison and disease; and enemy-held territory where Japanese patrols tried to lead them astray with false beacons. It was a flight that took them over the world's highest, most treacherous mountain range — to the rough, hand-hewn runways at Kunming, painstakingly laid out by countless thousands of Chinese coolies. And often, after these intrepid ATC pilots had completed their treacherous journey, they found that the landing field was underwater and/or closed in by clouds.

Many times the pilots took the less direct route, farther to the northwest, flying an additional 200 miles to avoid the enemy-held territory. They crossed the Hump at from 16,000 to 18,000 feet. In bad weather, however, the minimum was 20,000 feet, at which altitude the wings and control surfaces iced up.

All of this was accomplished despite the annual eight months of torrential, tropical downpours known as monsoons, which are followed by four months of violent, turbulent windstorms, capable in extremes of lifting or dropping a plane 6,000 to 8,000 feet in a minute. To top it all, these missions were flown by crews suffering from malaria and dysentery. (It was estimated officially that less than 60 per cent of the personnel would be effective after a year, and less than 30 per cent, six months later.) However, even if the weather happened to be good, and by some chance the crew happened to be in good health, the unarmed cargo planes — the C-46 Curtiss Commando and the Douglas C-47 affectionately known as the "Gooney Bird" — were still vulnerable to attack from Jap Zero fighter planes.

Through all of these trials and sufferings, the hard-pressed India-China Wing was successively commanded by Generals Alexander, Hoag, and Tunner. The last, Gen. William H. Tunner, stressed safety and efficiency and made the Hump operation the greatest airlift in history — up to that time. He later topped his own record in commanding the famous Berlin Airlift and the supplying of the United Nations Forces in the Korean conflict. General Tunner succeeded to the overall command of MATS from 1958 to 1960.

Together with Hannibal's crossing of the Alps, the Hump operation will go down in the annals of military history as one of the most difficult logistic missions accomplished by any military force. Their task was nobly done, defying all reason and common sense, and it was accomplished by dint of sheer willpower alone.

During those bleak days of the war, any ATC crewmen who had flown the Hump could hold their heads high in the face of the friendly jibes from fighter and bomber combat crews. In fun, their tormentors swore that the initials ATC stood for *A*llergic *T*o *C*ombat and in good humor they sang, "Take down your service flag, Mother. Your son's in the ATC."

In the beginning there had been very few who believed that the job could be done. Even the Japanese High Command refused to consider them a threat, doubting that they could even lift 1,000 tons a month to China. But the Army Air Corps' Air Transport Command had done it – and a lot more besides.

CHAPTER TWO

When the Chips Are Down-Humanitarian and Military Global Airlifts

WHAT IS A *normal* MATS operation like? Well, there is no such word as "normal" in the MATS dictionary. A normal, uneventful operation would be a rare exception to the usual MATS rule. If it wasn't an earthquake in Chile or a typhoon in Japan, then it was sure to be a "brush-fire" war in Indochina, trouble in Lebanon, aggression in the Formosa Strait, a disturbance in the Congo, or some other "normal" situation somewhere else in the world.

And more often than not, these disturbances come one on top of the other — they overlap. But MATS is flexible and takes them as they come — either one at a time, or two or more together. It was that way from the time MATS began in 1948.

The Berlin Airlift-"Operation Vittles"

The Soviet officer angrily shoved his chair away from the conference table and rose to his feet. His face was impassive and, as he strode from the room, the rows of medals on his chest swayed beneath the high-collared tunic of his Red Army uniform.

It was June 16, 1948. The place was the Kommandatura, the headquarters of the Allied governing body for occupied Berlin. The withdrawal of the Russian commandant signified the end of the Soviet participation in the Four-Power control — (American, British, French, and Russian) — of the city.

This decisive act had been preceded by months of constant pressure and indignities imposed by the Soviet Union — a Soviet "walkout" from the Allied Control Council in March, followed by a series of Red-imposed restrictions on transportation and communications in and out of West Berlin.

Exactly one week after the Soviet military commandant left the Kommandatura, the Soviets put a complete stop to freight traffic into West Berlin. They suspended parcel post service and cut off electric power. The following day, June 24, Soviet officials issued orders stopping all surface transportation and the movement of supplies into the western part of the city.

The total blockade of West Berlin had begun!

The Soviets were determined to force the Western Allies out of Berlin and starve the West Berliners into the Communist orbit.

They tore up tracks and closed the railroad freight routes. They stopped barge traffic on the rivers, destroyed bridges, and blockaded the *autobahn* (German express highway) and other roads.

West Berlin was completely isolated — an island of freedom 110 miles within the Soviet Zone.

But — what about the air? On that score, the Reds hadn't reckoned with the determination of the Western Allies. Britain, France, and the United States still had access rights to Berlin through three designated 20-mile-wide corridors.

Would the Russians try to stop them? How could they? Would they risk a third world war by trying to shoot them down? Anyhow, could the Western Powers possibly bring in enough food, coal, medicines, water, and other essentials by air to sustain the beleaguered city?

As for the Reds, they doubted it. It couldn't be done!

It was Sunday, June 26, when the historic Berlin Airlift got under way. Few of the participants — the pilots, crews, and the two million West Berliners — can forget it. (Nor, for that matter, can the Russians or the rest of the world.) Most could tell you precisely what they were doing at the moment they heard the news. The Germans called it *Luftbruecke,* or "air bridge," but officially it was known as "Operation Vittles."

Barely two days after the blockade had begun, the first military air transports began to arrive in West Berlin, loaded to capacity with the needed supplies. That same day the wires literally crackled as orders went out to the U.S. Air Force's Military Air Transport Command and Troop Carrier Command units around the globe. Soon MATS transports, which had been on routine or regularly scheduled flights, were winging their way toward Germany from Alaska, Japan, the Philippines, Hawaii, Australia, the Azores, England, and the United States. Organized only a scant four weeks before, MATS was about to perform the function for which it was created — it was undertaking the biggest strategic airlift job in history.

The first day's operations fell to the responsibility of Gen. Curtis E. LeMay's U.S. Air Force in Europe (USAFE). Using the only transport aircraft they had — the twin-engine Douglas C-47's — they delivered 80 tons of milk, flour, and medicine — all on that first day. The C-47 transport, known fondly as the "Gooney Bird," was a veteran of the Hump operation in World War II. As the civilian model DC-3, these planes had also been the workhorses of the commercial airlines since the early 1930's.

Within a week, MATS and TCC four-engine C-54 Skymasters were beginning to take up the task, and the tonnage volume of supplies began to move up.

By sweating and straining they were able to haul 384 tons for a 24-hour period ending on June 29. That day, three days after the lift had begun, the operations officer predicted that by July 20 they would be carrying 1,500 tons a day. His fellow pilots thought that he was completely out of his mind! They knew what an overbearing task it had been to haul a quarter of that amount into Berlin. But again they did the impossible. In two weeks, on July 15, five days ahead of schedule, they exceeded the estimate by flying 1,530 tons to the besieged city.

Nobody in their right mind would have ever believed that they would soon be flying 5,000 tons a day, and that even that lofty figure would be exceeded.

On July 23, MATS was ordered to take over the direction of the airlift and a few days later, the MATS Deputy Commander, Maj. Gen. William H. Tunner, established his headquarters at Wiesbaden, Germany.

To many of the pilots and crews, the route to Berlin was a familiar one. They had flown it before in B-17 Flying Fortresses, B-24 Liberators, B-25 Mitchells, and B-26 Marauders, with heavy bombloads to pulverize the Nazi capital. Others had flown that same route in P-51 Mustangs, P-47 Thunderbolts, and P-38 Lightnings, flying protective fighter cover for the bombers.

But this was a different kind of mission. It was "Operation Vittles," and the loads they were flying now were bringing life to that selfsame city, instead of destruction.

What was it like flying the Berlin Airlift? Well, as any pilot who did will tell you: "It was no picnic."

Imagine, if you can, rows of giant Skymasters with their cargo hatches wide open and large 10-ton Army trailer trucks backed up to them. Busily engaged loading each aircraft are volunteer teams of DP's (displaced persons from Latvia, Estonia, Poland, etc.). Supervising the loading and making certain that the weight is properly distributed and lashed down is an Air Force noncom. Also bustling about are the plane's ground crew.

The first of the flying crew to arrive is the flight engineer who inspects the plane. Next, the pilot and copilot, who have already been briefed on weather, navigation, and intelligence – that is, Soviet fighter plane activity in or near the Corridor. They too make an inspection of the aircraft.

With the loading completed, the pilot calls the tower for instructions. The tower checks with the Frankfurt Flight Control Center and relays the plane's departure time and altitude assignment back to it. This information is vital. It gives the pilot his particular spot in the lift.

The planes flew at five different altitudes, starting at 5,000 feet. All of the C-54's at the same altitude were 15 minutes apart. The next layer of aircraft were 500 feet above them and so on until the fifth level were at 7,000 feet. Since the planes at each altitude level were 15 minutes apart, by simple arithmetic (dividing the five levels into 15 minutes), we get a 3-minute interval between aircraft landing at Tempelhof Airport in West Berlin. Obviously, then, to avoid disastrous collisions in the crowded narrow corridors and the bustling airport, precision and timing were extremely important.

Now the pilot swings his plane around and taxis onto the long line of C-54's slowly inching their way to the takeoff position.

While waiting his turn, the pilot goes over his flight checklist with the copilot and flight engineer.

"Cowl flaps open?"

"Open."

"Tank selectors on main?"

"On main."

And so on down the list.

Twenty minutes after taxiing onto the line, the pilot had pushed the throttle forward and the Skymaster's powerful engines began to throb. Now they surge and rapidly pull the plane ahead and slowly lift it into the air. The pilot follows his takeoff heading until he reaches 900 feet and then turns toward Darmstadt, climbing at about

350 feet per minute at 160 mph. After flying 22 miles he swings around the Aschaffenburg Beacon and heads for the Fulda Range — the last directional guide this side of the Soviet Zone, and the last one until he gets to Berlin.

As he approaches Fulda, he can hear the next pilot, preceding him, reporting in. Our pilot checks his watch to make certain that he is in his proper position — three minutes behind. Precisely over Fulda he, in turn, reports so that the plane behind him can also check his position.

From this point, he's "on his own" and must guide himself by dead reckoning, all the while maintaining his assigned altitude and the indicated airspeed of 170 mph. Needless to say, there was always the danger of veering off course out of the narrow 20-mile-wide corridor, and so violating the restricted Soviet airspace.

Exactly forty minutes after reporting in at Fulda, the pilot tunes into the Tempelhof Field Control Station at Berlin and gets an altimeter setting and time check. Now he has five more control points to hit before he avoids the seven-story apartment house at the edge of the field, and finally touches down at Tempelhof.

Led by a "Follow Me" Jeep, the pilot guides his big plane to a designated station, where an unloading crew of Berliners is waiting for his priceless cargo. As he pulls up, a Post Exchange truck, with coffee and doughnuts, races up, followed by another car with a weather and an operations officer to brief him for his return trip, and a truck with a maintenance crew, ready to make any necessary emergency repairs. Shortly, he'll be winging his way back, ready to repeat the operation and bring another load in to Berlin.

What was it like? That was all there was to it — provided, of course, that the weather was good, no mechanical failures had occurred, and they hadn't been buzzed by Soviet Yak fighters.

At the height of "Operation Vittles," MATS alone had 4,000 officers and men and 300 C-54's (including some TCC aircraft) on the Berlin run. Nineteen more were used for training crews in a simulated Frankfurt-to-Berlin route — in the United States. Each of the planes flying the Berlin course was staffed with three crews. And this total did not include the U.S. Air Force C-47's and the Royal Air Force Yorks and Dakotas (also C-47's), and other miscellaneous aircraft.

Also not included in this total were the squadrons of Constellations (C-121's) and Globemasters (C-74's) that flew the supplies from the continental United States to Frankfurt, at which point the Berlin Airlift took over. Many thousands of miles of routes were covered by MATS and its Civilian Contract Carriers, Navy and Merchant ships, and Army Transportation Corps vehicles — to "feed" that short payoff stretch of a little more than 200 miles to Berlin.

It may be coincidental that the word "ton" is similar to "Tunner," but in air transport circles it was taken for granted. General Tunner was confident that the Berlin Airlift could have continued to deliver many tons of goods to West Berlin, forever. "We'll fly Vittles as long as the United States government wants it flown," he said.

But on May 12, 1949, eleven months after they imposed their restrictions, the Russians lifted the blockade. "Operation Vittles," however, continued, gradually tapering off in the early fall.

From the start of the blockade until August 1, 1949, the Berlin Airlift accomplished a Herculean task. They flew a massive 2,231,600 tons into that city, averaging a fantastic rate of 5,579 tons a day. They made a total of 275,544 flights for an average of better than 700 flights a day — a monumental achievement indeed!

As President Kennedy said some twelve years later, when the Soviets again tried to isolate West Berlin, they "intend to bring to an end . . . our legal rights to be in West Berlin, and, secondly, our ability to make good on our commitment to the two million free people of that city. That we cannot permit."

MATS did not permit it in 1948. They will not permit it today!

Dien Bien Phu-"Wounded Warrior"

A group of French Foreign Legionnaires lay on the ground. Dirty, bloody bandages covered head and other body wounds. Some had missing limbs, some were moaning, and some were dying.

These Legionnaires were casualties in a war against Communist aggression. In the past, defeat was not a word in common usage in the legendary Foreign Legion, but this was the dismal situation they faced in 1954.

The place was a besieged fort at Dien Bien Phu, in what was then Indochina. The Legionnaires were under constant devastating artillery fire from the heavy guns of the Red Vietminh guerrillas emplaced in the hills surrounding the perimeter of the fort. A ragged blue, white, and red tricolor still fluttered over this last feeble French outpost in the Far East. More accurately, Dien Bien Phu represented, symbolically if not heroically, the end of the once glorious French Empire. Yet, for the Legion, which consisted of Germans, Czechs, Poles, Hungarians, Americans, Englishmen, Russians, and a sprinkling of Frenchmen, it was a long way from the traditional Foreign Legion home at Sidi-bel-Abbès, Algeria, in North Africa.

It was a long way home indeed!

But at the request of the French government, the U.S. Military Air Transport Service flew the wounded Legionnaires over 14,000 miles — more than two-thirds of the way around the world — back to North Africa and to France. As the crow flies, the trip to France from Indochina is considerably shorter, but for political expediency, MATS was obliged to fly them the other way. They went from Saigon to Tokyo, over the Pacific Ocean and continental United States, and finally across the Atlantic to Paris or to Oran.

MATS had planned on evacuating some 1,000 Legionnaires but a change of plan necessitated airlifting a total of 509 of the wounded. Included in this group were 331 litter cases. The balance were ambulatory patients, able to get aboard the aircraft and to walk and get along with considerably less help.

"Operation Wounded Warrior," as it was called, was carried out in ten complete missions. A typical "run" went something like this:

The wounded soldiers were taken by Japan-based U.S. Far East Air Force C-124's from Saigon to Tokyo. At Tokyo they were fed and briefed on the "overwater" journey ahead of them, and then were helped aboard the MATS C-97. At each of the subsequent stops, at Hickam Field in Hawaii, Travis in California, and Westover in Massachusetts, there were layovers of fifteen hours so that the evacuees would have time to rest. This portion of the journey was handled by MATS' Pacific Division. The Atlantic Division took over at Westover Air Force Base, and took their wounded charges over the Atlantic, to France or Algeria. In today's Military Air Transport Service organization, the Pacific Division is known as WESTAF (Western Transport Air Force) and the Atlantic Division is called EASTAF (Eastern Transport Air Force).

From start to finish the entire mission took less than a month. It began on June 26, 1954, with MATS taking over from the Far East Air Force on June 29. The last trip was completed on July 17, at Orly airport in Paris. Three of the other trips had terminated in Paris and the remaining six in Oran.

Three types of military transports were used to accomplish this humanitarian mission. These consisted of Douglas C-124 Globemasters, Boeing C-97 Stratofreighters, and Douglas C-118 Liftmasters, as well as the MATS R6D's, the Navy designation for the Air Force C-118.

"Wounded Warrior" was the longest mercy mission in the history of the Military Air Transport Service. It brought to MATS the thanks and appreciation of a grateful France and the new nation of Vietnam. It also brought the undying devotion and gratitude of one of the world's greatest, most picturesque, gallant fighting forces – the French Foreign Legion.

Suez-United Nations Police Force

After numerous border violations and aggressions against them, the troops of the new state of Israel attacked. Knifing across the Egyptian border, they routed the soldiers of dictator Gamal Abdel Nasser. Administering a sound trouncing to the Egyptian *felahin* who fled before them, the well-disciplined Israeli army continued to drive through the Sinai Peninsula toward the Suez Canal. There was no opposition. Egyptian officers and soldiers threw away their weapons and ran or surrendered in droves. It was a total rout. Mountains of arms and equipment that had been supplied to the Egyptians by the Soviet Union were captured by the victorious Israeli army.

Then England and France joined the fight, jumping in to side with tiny Israel.

But, at the eleventh hour, the United States acted, calling for an end to the war and admonishment for England, France, and Israel.

At this point the cease-fire and police action became a United Nations affair. Again MATS, the good right arm of United States diplomacy, took over its function of delivering UN troops to Egypt.

As always, a MATS operation is a global operation. This one was no exception. Immediately after the United Nations decision had been made to place their own police force in the Suez Canal zone, MATS was called upon to perform the major portion of the long airlift. Responding instantly on November 9, 1956, two Lockheed C-121 Super Constellations left the MATS base at Charleston, South Carolina, to make the necessary preparations for carrying the advance party of Colombian troops from South America. One of the C-121's brought staging crews to Ramey Air Force Base in Puerto Rico. These were to serve as relief crews for the "Connies" arriving from Bogotá on the first leg of the journey to the staging area in Capodichino, Italy. At the second stop on the long trip — the MATS installation at Lajes Field in the Azores — relief crews were ready and waiting.

Meanwhile, the second C-121 was on its way from Charleston to Bogotá, Colombia, carrying the necessary control teams for operations, traffic, and maintenance, as well as other supporting personnel. The latter were charged with the responsibility of checking such things as airfields, runway lengths, communications facilities, tower control, lighting, and the suitability of the available local aviation gasoline. It was their decision to use the Palenquero Airfield for "onloading" the main force of Colombian troops, rather than Bogotá. And the data gathered by the control team was used to brief all incoming flights.

Soon the other MATS "Connie" arrived and the fifty-five officers and men of the Colombian army advance party were manifested, onloaded, and the plane was airborne and on its way to Ramey, Puerto Rico; Lajes in the Azores; and Naples, Italy.

Then, with the completion of the airlift of this relatively small advance party, MATS was suddenly taken off the "alert status." It looked as though all of the preplanning and physical preparations for the larger mission had gone for nothing. Less than a day went by, however, when they were ordered to reschedule the flights through Khartoum in the Sudan to the USAF base in Dhahran, Saudi Arabia. The purpose was to make them available for the airlift of Indian troops from Agra as well.

Soon the Colombian airlift was in full swing again, but not to Khartoum and Dhahran, according to the amended plan; rather, it was going to be to Capodichino in Naples, as originally scheduled. In the Colombian portion of the Suez Airlift, the Military Air Transport Service carried a total of 585 soldiers and 35,000 pounds of baggage.

While all of this was going on, the Indian airlift materialized and the big MATS C-121's, with their distinctive triple stabilizers, took off to accomplish this new mission. In addition to the "Connies," C-124 Globemasters were diverted from the regular across-the-Atlantic "channel" run to the USAF cargo base at Châteauroux, France, and then rerouted from Dover AFB in Delaware to Wheelus, Tripoli; Dhahran; and on to Agra, India. Once at Agra, the MATS crews learned that each Globemaster would have to carry 31,000 pounds on every trip. This, in itself, presented no great problem. What did present a problem, however, was that the lift included thirty passengers for each plane. Since these were nonpressurized cargo aircraft and carried no oxygen for passengers, they were forced to fly well below their practical operating ceiling. This prevented them from flying the shorter northern route and necessitated returning the way that they had come – through Dhahran and Khartoum. The heavy loads, however, required the scheduling of trips through Khartoum in the early morning – before the sun reached its zenith, with the accompanying intense heat. The C-124's would have found it difficult taking off in the high temperature.

In one part of the operation, two R7V's (Super Constellations of the MATS Navy component) traveled more than 20,000 nautical miles from Hickam Field in Hawaii to Agra, India. From here they picked up the Indian soldiers and cargo, and then flew on to Capodichino, Italy. They finished the trip back to Hawaii by completely circling the globe. Although the entire trip lasted ten days, one of the aircraft made the "round-the-world" trip in well under four days' actual flying time.

Despite all kinds of problems and obstacles, including typhoons, MATS completed the airlift of Indian troops for the United Nations shortly before the close of 1956. In all, the Indian part of the airlift carried close to 1,000 soldiers and 275,000 pounds of cargo. This included the soldiers' baggage, arms and equipment, food, medical supplies, tents, water purification equipment, and other impedimenta.

Once again MATS proved that it was made of the proper ingredients to provide "instant airlift."

Hungary–"Safe Haven"

The lead tank rolled into the Budapest square, pivoted to the side on one track, and stopped. It was a Soviet heavy tank – a Josef Stalin III – and its big turret, bearing a Red star on each side, continued to rotate, the massive cannon and machine gun passing along the massed crowd of Hungarians lining the square. Like a giant finger it moved, as though pointing at each one, singling him out and serving a personal warning.

Then, the rest of the tank column pulled into the square.

The Hungarians had revolted against Soviet rule in 1956 and after a bloody battle the Russians had pulled out leaving the "Freedom Fighters" in control.

But now the Soviets had returned—and in strength. The taste of freedom had been short-lived. Thousands of Hungarian families fled the country by whatever means they could. They went by foot, bicycle, car, and hay wagon. Most of them stole across the border into Austria. Here, however, there were few facilities for them and the situation was getting more desperate as each day went by.

In its traditional role as haven and home for the oppressed, the United States agreed to accept 21,500 of these Hungarian refugees. Of this number, MATS had the responsibility of flying 9,700. Included were 139 escapees who required special aeromedical evacuation.

MATS, which had just completed its airlift in support of the United Nations in Suez, was ordered to undertake "Operation Safe Haven" on December 9, 1956. In less than two days the first MATS aircraft, a C-118, loaded with fifty Hungarian refugees, had roared off the runway at Munich-Riem Airport in Germany, on its way to the United States and freedom.

One hundred and fifty-five flights later, on January 3, 1957, another MATS Liftmaster flew in the last load of escapees to McGuire Air Force Base in New Jersey. During this 22-day period, MATS had fulfilled its mission, flying in its allotted quota of 9,700 Hungarian men, women, and children. With Phase I completed during the 3-week period, MATS went on to Phase II and by the end, on June 20, 1957, had boosted the total to 14,263.

This turned out to be the greatest peacetime airlift of civilians ever accomplished. And the entire operation was carried out without a single accident or mishap. Indeed, the name "Operation Safe Haven" was appropriate for more reasons than one.

"Safe Haven" was accomplished by the officers and airmen of MATS who worked night and day, even through the Christmas and New Year holidays. They were supported by U.S. Army personnel who also worked around the clock to provide the refugees with food, shelter, medical treatment, and processing at both the European and U.S. ends of the lift. Together they gave their Hungarian charges the very best Christmas gift anyone could ever receive—*freedom!*

President Eisenhower expressed it this way:

"Thus, we welcome you to American soil. We realize that you ardently hope for a time when all Hungarians can enjoy the blessings of individual freedom in their Hungarian mother-country. We join in that hope. And we give you this present assurance — if, when that day dawns once more, you should choose to go back to your native homes in Hungary, America will do its best in helping you to return."

Some 65 MATS aircraft participated in this humanitarian airlift. In addition to the C-118 Liftmasters, there were the big C-121 Lockheed Super Constellations, easily recognized by their distinctive bank of triple stabilizers, and the R6D's, the Navy version of the C-118. Also included were the planes of eleven commercial airlines that were under contract to the Military Air Transport Service for this operation.

Lebanon

Then it happened!

President Eisenhower received an urgent call for help from the Middle East in 1958. That tiny country, Lebanon — half Moslem and half Christian — was being threatened by a new form of indirect aggression. Sorely needed troops and supplies had to be airlifted to Lebanon as soon as possible. And it also had to be done without public knowledge, so as not to inform a possible enemy of the deployment of our troops.

Instantly the call went out for a task force of 36 MATS Globemasters to report to Rhein-Main in Germany — within 36 hours. Considering the fact that the practical flying time from the United States to Europe, for the C-124, is 30 hours (including necessary stops for refueling), the deadline was an exceedingly close one.

The aircraft that flew in to join this Lebanon Airlift were actually based at Donaldson AFB, South Carolina; Larson AFB, Washington; and Dover, Delaware. MATS, with its global communications system, however, was able to catch them "on the wing" and divert this so-called "air alert force" from England, France, and the Azores in short order.

The first C-124 was at Rhein-Main in less than five hours, and the entire task force was in full operation two hours *before* the deadline. And within that period some of the Globemasters had already delivered their precious cargo to the eastern shores of the Mediterranean Sea.

MATS Headquarters at Scott Air Force Base, Illinois.

The giant Lockheed 7-141 Starlifter, one of the newest additions to MATS' inventory of strategic airlift craft.

A veteran in olive drab of World War II and the historic "Hump" operation, the C-47 Skytrain became one of the first MATS aircraft when the service absorbed the wartime Air Transport Command.

Douglas Aircraft Co.

Chinese troops tackle the "Hump." During the famous World War II airlift, commanded by Brig. Gen. Turner, Chinese troops scramble aboard a C-46 aircraft of the Air Transport Command, later to become MATS.

Once at Tempelhof Airport in Berlin, the big planes fall into line and are systematically "offloaded."

Gen. Clay and USAF and RAF officers look over a model layout showing the "onloading" operation for the Berlin Airlift. Trucks bring the coal and other supplies from the railroad cars on the siding to the waiting air transports.

German children watch the seemingly never-ending parade of MATS C-54s flying into Tempelhof airport in Berlin.

Finally the Soviets, seeing that there wasn't much they could do to prevent the aerial supply of the city, lifted the blockade of West Berlin and "Operation Vittles" came to an end.

Troops from Colombia, South America being airlifted in a MATS C-121 Constellation to Naples, Italy, on their way to Suez as part of the United Nations Police Force.

"Welcome to Lebanon," says the sign on the administration building at the airport in Beirut. And welcome indeed were the 5,400 American troops and 5,500 tons of cargo airlifted there in support of the Lebanese government.

Like the whale that swallowed Jonah, a MATS C-124 Globemaster swallows a Tactical Air Command F-104 Starfighter. During the crisis in 1958 MATS airlifted, in this fashion, an entire fighter squadron of F-104s, together with its planes, pilots, ground crews, and maintenance equipment to Formosa.

Other members of the United Nations force form up after debarking from a C-130 Hercules. These Swedish troops had been airlifted from their homeland to the Congo.

U.S. Marines being briefed at Guantanamo Bay in the shadow of the MATS aircraft that just brought them from the United States.

U.S. Navy Photo

Ready for three weeks in the field, these troops of the Army's 2nd Armored Division from Texas step off the MATS C-135 jet at Rhein-Main in the deployment phase of Exercise "Big Lift."

Troops of the 2nd Armored Division of Fort Hood, Texas, taking part in Exercise "Big Lift" in Germany, disembark from a MATS Service C-135 at Ramstein Air Base, Germany.

A C-124 Globemaster taking on two Air Force buses.

This task force furnished a strategic airlift to Lebanon for more than two months. The roar of the C-124 engines, as they swooped over the mosques and minarets, mingled with the voices of the Muzzeins calling the faithful to prayer. In all, the MATS crews flew over 7,000 flying hours, transporting some 5,000 passengers and more than 5,000 tons of supplies.

When the threat to Lebanon was neutralized, the United States soldiers, sailors, and Marines pulled out, along with MATS.

Summing up the Lebanon operation, President Eisenhower said:

> "Two great lessons have been taught. First, the United States is a friend to those who wish to live their own lives in freedom. We are not deterred by threats or abuse from giving needed help. Second, the United States never seeks to turn the necessities of others into gains for itself. . . ."

Formosa and "Operation Jonah Able"

While all of this was going on in Lebanon and elsewhere in the world, the alarm bell rang again in August of 1958.

The Chinese Communists were shelling Quemoy and threatening Matsu. These tiny islands in the Straits of Formosa are the closest Nationalist territory to the mainland of China. Under heavy artillery fire, the Reds appeared to be softening up the little islands preparatory to an invasion. Again it was time to act. The U.S. Air Force's Tactical Air Command (TAC) was ordered to organize and send a Composite Air Strike Force to Formosa. This combined force consisted of jet fighters and bombers.

Once more MATS marshaled its forces to support the operation. Again, as in the Lebanon Airlift, there was no public announcement so as not to alert a possible enemy concerning our troop movements. Originally MATS had planned on 36 airlift trips operating out of three bases in the United States. However, this was increased to 80 trips from seven bases. But what was more important, shortly after the order was issued the striking force was at its destination — ready for action!

Although the operation was a complete success, there seemed to be one oversight. No F-104's were among the jet fighters sent to Formosa. This Starfighter was our latest, most modern, supersonic jet fighter. Called "the missile with a man in it," this Century Series fighter flies at 1,400 miles per hour – twice the speed of sound. So formidable a weapon was this that our military leaders felt we should have some of them on Taiwan – and that they should be there "yesterday"!

But how to get them there? The little jet fighters have only a short range. By the longest stretch of their capabilities (and of the imagination), they could never span the vast Pacific Ocean. The urgency of the situation and the need for speed ruled out transportation by ship.

There was only one way – MATS was the answer!

Quick as a wink, MATS C-124's flew into Hamilton Air Force Base near San Francisco. There they were met by a squadron of Starfighters.

Do you remember the Bible story of how Jonah was swallowed by the whale and how he lived in the whale's belly and was eventually delivered? Well, "Operation Jonah Able" was the modern, multiple version of that Old Testament story.

Like some giant sea monster, the massive Globemaster stood with its jaws wide open. A "double take" was needed to make certain that your eyes weren't deceiving you. Yet, sure enough, the cavernous mouth of the MATS cargo aircraft was devouring, whole, a USAF jet fighter – a Lockheed F-104.

Not only did the Globemasters swallow the entire squadron of Starfighters, they also carried the fighters' pilots, ground crews, and maintenance equipment along and delivered them intact to Formosa. This operation marked a historical milestone in the annals of air transportation. It was the first time that a *complete* operational Air Force squadron was airlifted in a single-package operation.

During the Formosan crisis, MATS made 144 trips and ferried close to 2,000 passengers and 2,000 tons of equipment. And the Starfighters they delivered may well have deterred another Communist aggression.

Congo

Taxiing down the runway at Léopoldville, the C-124 MATS Globemaster pulled up alongside of a big four-engine turboprop. Toward the rear of the foreign aircraft, below the rudder, were the large letters CCCP, which is the Cyrillic (or Russian) script for U.S.S.R. Along the center of the fuselage were the symbols which stood for "Aeroflot" – the Soviet state airline. In the United States, Aeroflot would be equivalent to a combination of MATS and all of the U.S. commercial airlines put together. In the Soviet Union there are no privately owned airlines. Aeroflot takes care of both civil and military air transport.

This Soviet aircraft was an Il-18, which flies at the same speed as the Hercules. It was one of five of this type of plane reportedly participating in the United Nations airlift to the Congo, along with the numerous MATS C-124 and C-130 Hercules turboprops of the USAFE 322nd Air Division. In November, 1962, jet C-135's joined the operation.

Despite the small number of Soviet transport aircraft in the Congo operation, it marked their first participation in a United Nations strategic airlift. It made this mission a true United Nations endeavor. For, in addition to the Pakistani troops and equipment that were brought in by the MATS C-124 that was taxiing down the runway at Léopoldville, other MATS aircraft had already airlifted a miniature United Nations of troops directly from their homelands to the Congo. They carried soldiers from Ireland, Ghana, Morocco, Guinea, Ethiopia, India, the United Arab Republic, Nigerian Tunisia, Sweden, Indonesia, and more.

Not only did MATS fly in troops and their equipment, they also airlifted badly needed food to the Congo. For example, four of the giant C-130 turboprops carried 200,000 pounds of dried fish more than 4,000 miles, from Flesland, Norway, to Luluabourg, during the last week of January, 1961. This was only a small part of the more than 1,100 tons of food ferried into the Congo by Military Air Transport Service C-124's and C-130's at that time.

What was all of this activity in the Congo?

In the heart of Africa, the shouts and joys of Congolese independence were short-lived. The Belgians, who had ruled over the Congo for eighty years, after much pressure and coercion had finally relinquished control. However, most of the 14 million Congolese were primitive people, poorly educated and ill prepared to govern themselves. The internal political struggle between rival political factions led to armed revolt, fighting, and bloodshed. The newly found freedom turned independence into mass confusion, a bloodbath and massacre of the former white *rulers,* the rise of a Communist force, and the secession of Katanga Province – the richest area in the Congo with practically all of the mineral wealth. On July 14, 1960, just one week after the Congo had been admitted into membership, it became necessary for the world organization to act.

And again MATS swung into action!

During that first week, the Air Force had thrown 40 C-130's and 36 MATS C-124's into the operation, and was reinforcing with 24 more of the giant transports. In this initial phase of the airlift they carried more than 4,000 troops from five different nations, in addition to thousands of tons of food and equipment. Included in these shipments flown in by MATS were such items as communications facilities, maintenance equipment, helicopters, liaison planes, and even complete mess halls. At some points the airlift was a two-way shuttle — ferrying in UN soldiers and flying out returning Belgian troops, or UN troops that had been replaced, to their homelands. MATS also made emergency trips, flying the 663 nautical miles from Léopoldville to Stanleyville, and back, to rescue threatened refugees.

Meanwhile the C-124 that had just landed at Léopoldville had disembarked its complement of Pakistani soldiers. Having departed from the big USAF cargo base at Châteauroux, France, the aircraft and crew, at the completion of their journey, will have covered some 14,000 miles and will have been away just short of 56½ hours before returning to their home base.

Here is the story of that C-124's flight from the beginning:

As the pilot pulled the control column toward his chest, the big Globemaster lifted off the runway at Châteauroux and headed southeast toward Italy. The pilot, a major with fifteen years' experience, was a veteran of the Berlin Airlift and the numerous other MATS strategic operations. He settled back about his duties. The C-124 carried eight other crew members, including copilot, navigator, flight engineer, and load master. For the Congo emergency some of these men were on temporary duty, from Donaldson Air Force Base in South Carolina.

Passing over a layer of wispy white clouds, they could make out the farms and tiny villages of southern France in the early morning sun. Before long these gave way to the blue Mediterranean, and finally the toe of the Italian boot passed beneath the wings.

The navigator looked up from his radar set and indicated a heading toward Cairo. Crossing the Mediterranean they were soon over the Gulf of Suez and bearing out over that vast expanse of sand that is the great Nafud Desert. But soon they were across it and landing at the great "oasis" — the big USAF air base at Dhahran, Saudi

Arabia. There they found welcome food, drink, and rest, as well as fuel and maintenance for their aircraft, before taking off again for Karachi to pick up their passengers and cargo.

By the afternoon of the second day the Globemaster was settling down on the runway at Karachi. Soon Pakistani troops, looking very British in berets and coveralls, were stowing their gear aboard under the watchful eye of the MATS load master. And in short order, the full Pakistani contingent was smartly marching aboard to the tune of Scottish bagpipes.

Airborne again, the big plane headed back toward Dhahran – to spend the night at the "oasis" before shoving off for the Sudan and Khartoum. Taking off the following day from Khartoum, they could see the pattern of the streets laid out in the arrangement of the British Union Jack by Lord Kitchener in the late nineteenth century.

Next stop, Léopoldville! Soon after the Globemaster had taxied up alongside of the Russian Il-18, the Pakistani troops debarked and off-loaded their baggage. The MATS task for this particular mission was completed. They had delivered a contingent of soldiers to the Congo for the UN Police Force.

Now, the job was to get back home.

Leaving the Congo, the transport headed northwest, over Equatorial Africa toward Kano, Nigeria. There was a slight delay while the flight engineer earned his keep – one of the four big engines was in need of emergency repairs, and he got to work on it. Soon the Globemaster was aloft again, bearing due north, 1,500 miles over the Sahara Desert, to Wheelus AFB in Tripoli.

Having refueled, the Globemaster was now on the last leg of its trip. Leaving the coast of North Africa behind, it was only a short time until the blue Mediterranean sparkled below. Soon, the fabled Côte d'Azur – the southern coast of France – appeared in the distance. In rapid succession the tiny villages, vineyards, and farms of southern and central France were seen once more. Then the pilot eased up on the throttle for a power letdown. The flaps were down, the wheels lowered, and soon the plane touched down with a screech on the field at Châteauroux. The major reversed the pitch on his four giant propellers and the Globemaster slowed down to taxi into position.

Another MATS mission completed successfully!

But, another MATS mission was also ready to begin in the seemingly never ending task of global airlift!

Southeast Asia

Communist guerrillas had driven the Royal Laotian army before them and had captured two important cities. Now they were pushing toward the Mekong River which separates Laos from Thailand. The tiny nation of Thailand, fearing Red aggression across the river, called for help in May of 1962. And the United States was quick to furnish it.

The United States, under the terms of the Southeast Asia Treaty Organization, was meeting its defense obligations to Thailand. Soon 5,000 U.S. soldiers, Marines, and airmen began to arrive at Bangkok, the capital and principal port of the little country that was formerly known as Siam. Fourteen hundred Leathernecks of the 3rd Marine Division in camouflage battle dress streamed ashore from a naval transport ship. They were following another 400 Marine airmen ferried ashore by helicopter from the U.S. aircraft carrier *Valley Forge.*

It was the middle of spring and the start of the monsoon season. In order to do the job they were brought in for, the troops had to be airlifted to the Mekong River—and quickly! That's where MATS entered the picture.

The very same night MATS heavy air transports were taking off every fifteen minutes from Don Muang airport outside of Bangkok. Like an aerial shuttle, they carried the American military personnel to Udon some 300 miles to the northeast.

In short order the Americans were in position, ready for anything. Often, all that is necessary is to show that you are ready and willing to stand up to an aggressor. The cold, hard reality that our friendly troops had been brought by MATS to the place they were needed at the time they were needed, most probably saved the day.

The Communist guerrilla forces did not cross the Mekong.

This was the first large-scale landing of U.S. combat troops and the first in Southeast Asia since the Korean War. It paved the way for the 20,000 American military personnel, helicopters, and other massive aid furnished to Thailand's neighbor, South Vietnam, in its struggle against the Red Viet Cong forces.

Many of these Americans gave their lives in South Vietnam from 1962 through 1964 in the never ending battle against the enemy guerrillas.

CHAPTER THREE

Cuba, India, and Regular Routine-Six Weeks of World Crisis

As the U.S. global airlift command, MATS is geared to react instantaneously to international tension. In the preceding pages specific missions have been described. This chapter gives the overall MATS picture and the interaction and cooperation between the air transport divisions and the MATS technical services in performing missions for the Department of Defense during the historic six-week period — October 1 to November 15.

October of 1962 began as a fully scheduled month, a month where the MATS force would be exercised fully. Airlifts based on the known increase that could be expected over the preceding year, new requirements, plus recurring requirements already programmed, were to keep MATS very busy. These recurring requirements were the Army "Rotaplan" — rotation of combat troops to Europe and return; "Long Thrust V" — planned exercises for the support of NATO; Congo troop rotations of both Swedish and Irish United Nations soldiers; and "Southern Express" where Europe-based troops were taken to NATO maneuvers in Greece. Others were "Three Pairs," "Deep Freeze," "Blue Water," JTF-8 Support and Joint Airborne Training.

All of these requirements could be met — but with some strain — using normal crew duty hours and a normal flying rate per aircraft each day. It was expected to be a *full* month based on the records of the year past and the stated requirements of the other military services. In reality, however, when the reports were all in at the end of the month, hundreds of extra missions had been flown by MATS during this period.

This is the way it happened.

On October 1, the MATS big transports were already engaged in the airlift of relief supplies and equipment – tents and medical supplies out of Europe to Iran – Project IDA. This consisted of relief to the stricken Iranians hit by an earthquake. Army field hospitals were flown in and medical personnel deployed. In all, 443.8 tons of material and 17 missions were flown using C-133's and C-124's over a 3,300-mile route.

In addition, October 1 saw the beginning of Long Thrust V, a normal troop lift exercise for the Army – demonstrating NATO support by U.S. Army troops stationed in the United States. MATS took this in its stride by using conventional powered aircraft over a period of eighteen days. In this operation, over 17.3 tons of equipment and 1,362 troops were airlifted to Europe using 25 missions, and 1,133 troops and 38.9 tons were returned requiring 26 missions.

Blended into Long Thrust V, but not a part of it, was the Southern Express exercise. This meant that MATS airlift aircraft already in the European area were further used to airlift 470 tons and 3,000 troops from Europe to Greece for NATO maneuvers using 127 missions. Amazingly enough, MATS pilots accomplished it while waiting for their rotational trips back to the U.S. on the Long Thrust operation.

It is interesting to note that many MATS airlifts utilize this diversion principle. Skilled airlift traffic and operations people in the MATS Command Post at Scott Air Force Base, Illinois, work out loads both ways, or divert aircraft while away from home station to accomplish other immediate requirements, thus minimizing "deadheading" and increasing aircraft utilization rate. This, of course, is the practical and economical way to operate, but it is also hard on the crews. Not many personal plans can be made when the crews don't know when they will leave, what route they will take coming home – or even when they will get there.

Moreover, on October 1, MATS was engaged in the airlift of Army troops within the United States on various exercises, including "Project Rapid Road" – the airlift of 12,500 troops to the University of Mississippi during the integration crisis. The new Boeing C-135 Stratolifter jets and conventional MATS transports were used together during the first nine days of October to fly a total of 308 missions, transporting over 12,000 troops and 2,000 tons of cargo to points within continental United States.

On October 10 through 16, an all-jet C-135 Stratolifter airlift of

Swedish troops for the United Nations into the Congo was accomplished. This was the first all-jet airlift into the Congo. Sixteen point six tons and 1,232 troops were rotated from Stockholm to the Congo and return. This route was 4,900 statute miles long and each aircraft flew it nonstop in ten hours average. Four of the new jet transports were used in 19 missions.

By the eleventh, Project IDA — relief to Iran — Deep Freeze to Antarctica, Southern Express to Greece, Long Thrust V to Germany, and the United Nations deployment of Swedish troops to the Congo were all in high gear. This involved about half of the MATS airlift force.

On October 16, MATS began a wartime activity rate, as directed by the Joint Chief of Staff, because of the Cuban crisis. This was accomplished by increasing the authorized flying hours for each crew, by putting maintenance personnel on double shifts, and by maintaining an even closer watch over aircraft utilization. It included loading heavier loads. In short, the whole tempo of MATS was stepped up.

By the morning of October 17, an airlift of conventional ammunition for the Tactical Air Command, and their Composite Air Strike Force support equipment, began into Florida bases.

Four days later, on October 21, a historic airlift occurred. This was the first of many missions required to airlift Marines and their combat gear to Guantanamo Bay and the southeast United States. Marine ammunition and Marine fighter aircraft support, as well as the troops and their combat gear, were positioned in a short time.

On October 23, MATS lost the C-135 and crew engaged in the ammunition airlift to Guantanamo. This was the only loss during the whole period. All other MATS flight operations were accident-free.

During the period from October 16 to almost the end of the month, thousands of troops were moved and thousands of tons of cargo airlifted in hundreds of sorties. These flights operated throughout the world and were controlled from the MATS Command Post at headquarters in Scott Air Force Base.

Meanwhile, Long Thrust V, Congo, and Rotaplan were completed October 22. By now the full MATS global airlift had been mobilized for use by the Department of Defense in Cuba — if needed. However, conventional and routine requirements, laid on by MATS users, were not ignored or unduly delayed during this period. Even though much of the active MATS airlift force was withdrawn from the routine airlift requirements around the globe, the depot levels of priority freight did not get out of hand, nor were rotational passengers delayed.

How was this accomplished?

MATS contracted for commercial airlift to handle routine requests that had been programmed early in the month. Contracts were let with commercial airlines, but by October 25 it became apparent that no more outsize commercial aircraft were available — the airlines could not voluntarily supply anything more on commercial contracts. Immediately MATS took to monitoring the operational readiness of the Civil Reserve Air Fleet (CRAF), to insure its capability for maximum response — if it were needed.

At the same time actions were taken to increase the operational readiness of MATS Air National Guard and Reserve units. Two Guard units, recently released from active duty with MATS (the 133rd and 146th Air Transport Wings), even volunteered to take over the supply of cold country bases. They flew their Boeing C-97's on 29 missions to five locations and hauled 266 tons of cargo. And, like all Reserve and National Guard units, they did it on a volunteer basis, during training time.

These extraordinary MATS accomplishments did not go unnoticed.

Chief of Naval Operations Admiral George W. Anderson summed it up in his November message to General LeMay. He said, "Please accept the congratulations and appreciation of the Navy and the Marine Corps for the absolutely magnificent performance of MATS in positioning our Marines from the West Coast in Guantanamo.

"The efficiency and dispatch with which this operation was carried out attests to outstanding coordination and direction from the top down through and including the line mechanics for the individual aircraft.

"The Marine lift into Guantanamo was but one of the many MATS accomplishments during recent days, without which our combined efforts would have been something less than effective."

By the end of October, some MATS crews were able to check in at home to watch their kids dress for "trick or treat," but they were also sitting next to their telephones. The whole force remained on alert — key personnel never more than ten minutes from their phone — crews, fifteen minutes. Traffic, maintenance and inspection, and operations personnel on the flight line had no breather. Their work was to keep the force in flying condition. Duty for them was twelve hours on and twelve hours off, seven days a week.

Then came the next unexpected call. India! Here again it was obvious to the hardworking crews that the MATS forces were in the front lines of the cold war – taking to the air on minimum notice as an instrument of national policy.

On November 2, C-135 crews from McGuire and Travis Air Force Bases were airborne for Europe to airlift arms for India. This situation was made for the big new Boeing jets. Halfway around the globe with arms for the Indian army, with the ability built into the 500-mph Stratolifters – not only for quick reaction, but to be able to return to their own hemisphere with jet speed if their services were required in any other situation. This 12,000-mile-long airlift was accomplished in eight days.

The arms lift to India, however, did not represent the last of the pressure. On November 5, a rush airlift job of communications and electrical gear to La Paz, Bolivia, was called for. What at first appeared to be a routine "milk run" to assist a South American neighbor now posed some interesting airlift problems.

The airstrip at La Paz is at an altitude of 13,000 feet. The pay loads which are normal for the Douglas C-124 Globemasters and C-133 transports were too heavy to land at that altitude. This required a shuttle operation – landing the heavy loads at a lower field and then transshipping them into smaller loads in the C-124's. In this way, the Globemasters could make the difficult landing at La Paz.

Starting on November 7 and finishing on November 17 was another United Nations 4,900-mile troop rotation into the Congo. This time it was airlifting Irish troops from Dublin, Ireland, to Léopoldville in the Congo. It was done with eight C-118's and one C-133 – 45.1 tons and 696 troops down the long haul, and 16.7 tons and 581 personnel back to Ireland. Twenty-nine missions were required.

By this time – far into November – it looked again to the operations people like it might be a normal month. Special missions here and there, missions that could be planned in advance so that crews and aircraft could be programmed – but it wasn't to remain that way.

On November 13, still another interesting and unexpected airlift materialized. This one was to Venezuela, using a Douglas C-133 Cargomaster. The Creole Petroleum Company, Lake Maracaibo,

Venezuela, had become an early victim of Cuban Communist sabotage. The loss in oil revenues to the government of Venezuela was mounting up to millions of dollars per day. The State Department called on MATS, as possessors of the only aircraft large enough to airlift the big General Electric generators and switch gear, to fly the replacement material down to get the wells back in operation.

Also on November 13 came the requirements of a humanitarian-type airlift to Guam which MATS crews are regularly called upon to fly. A 175-mph typhoon had hit the island hours before. Relief in the form of blankets, tents, field kitchens, medical supplies, generators, and all sorts of emergency supplies were needed now. The first C-124's were en route to Guam in about two hours after the call. C-135's from Travis and McGuire, some just back from the India arms lift, took off immediately. By November 15 (the date of the end of this six-week period, but not the end of the Guam airlift), over 600 tons of emergency gear had been flown out the long over-water legs to Guam in 64 missions. Six thousand statute miles in about twelve hours' flying time in the jets.

Coming home in the C-135 jets by November 15 were over 800 homeless military dependents. Some with only the clothes on their backs. Helping them, too, was the MATS U.S. Air Force Aid Society fund. At least $5,000 had been given to them for emergency expenses, not including the expenditures of the Red Cross.

Before the Guam relief aircraft were all airborne, another call for help had to be answered. MATS C-124's with air cargo drop capability flew to the aid of an American scientific expedition spending the winter on an ice island 300 miles south of the North Pole. Twenty thousand pounds of fuel oil were needed. This was 1,800 miles north of Elmendorf Air Force Base in Alaska.

At the other pole, the Globemaster resupply of the Antarctic scientific stations, called Deep Freeze, started in early October, also continued. Nine hundred tons of fuel had been air-dropped by the end of the six-week period.

The missions described here, which represent a cross section of MATS activities for this period, result in some interesting totals — 13,029.4 tons (or 26,058,800 pounds) and 34,415 personnel were airlifted. In terms of rail transportation, this would require a train with 945 railroad cars over 10 miles long. Nor does this include the tonnage and passengers contracted to commercial carriers for routine air transportation.

Throughout these hectic six weeks, MATS had maintained the

combat readiness to support simultaneous or other Joint Chiefs of Staff approved war plans which might be related to the crisis. Moreover, MATS technical services were also engaged in a maximum effort.

For example, the Air Weather Service had an important role in supplying special weather analysis over the globe. This worldwide analysis was stepped up in addition to the "saturation" weather reporting required over the southeastern United States and Cuban area.

Weather forecasts in the southeastern United States and at sea around Cuba were supplied to the Air Photographic and Charting Service for reconnaissance photography, to the Tactical Air Command, to Army units, and to Naval units which also depended on weather ships in the area. Air Weather Service moved forecasters and observers to Florida bases. WB-50 aircraft and crews were moved from McClellan Air Force Base, California, to Kindley Air Force Base, Bermuda. Weather reconnaissance missions were flown around the periphery of Cuba twice a day. In addition, several hundred other forecasters and observers were on standby alert.

The Air Photographic and Charting Service, charged with the responsibility of documenting all Air Force activities, was also busy deploying combat photographers to operating locations to supply documentary film on the buildup in the southeastern United States. In addition, regular global activities were maintained. The 1370th Photo Mapping Wing relocated aircraft and men to aid in aerial photography over the Atlantic Ocean.

The MATS Air Rescue Service also had a terrific load to carry. Air Rescue Service forces provided daily precautionary coverage in support of reconnaissance and fighter missions by Tactical Air Command, Navy and Strategic Air Command aircraft. They provided actual search activities in an attempt to locate a downed SAC reconnaissance aircraft. And Air Rescue Service helicopters provided fire suppression and local base rescue support at five of the buildup bases.

Altogether Air Rescue Service provided aircraft, several hundred personnel, local base rescue detachments, and rescue squadrons. Many aircraft were on 24-hour alert. In addition, Air Rescue Service put other crews on standby for possible augmentation.

This is how MATS operates. And that is how it reacted to global tension from October 1 to November 15, 1962.

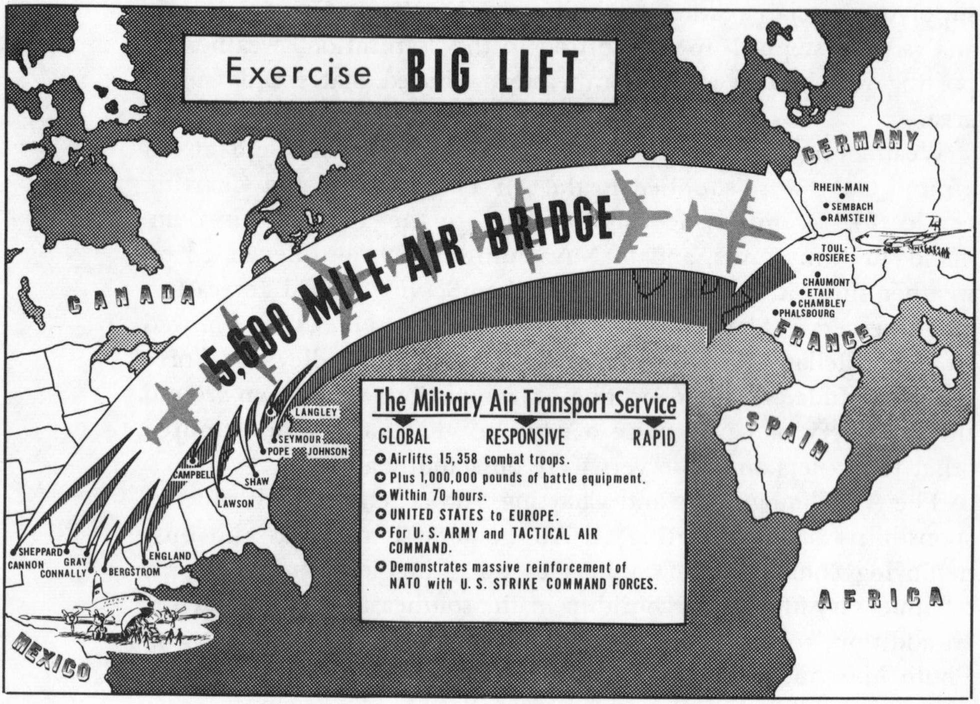

Exercise BIG LIFT
5,600 MILE AIR BRIDGE
CANADA
MEXICO
GERMANY
FRANCE
SPAIN
AFRICA
RHEIN-MAIN
SEMBACH
RAMSTEIN
TOUL-ROSIERES
CHAUMONT
ETAIN
CHAMBLEY
PHALSBOURG
LANGLEY
SEYMOUR
POPE
JOHNSON
CAMPBELL
SHAW
LAWSON
SHEPPARD
CANNON
GRAY
CONNALLY
BERGSTROM
ENGLAND
The Military Air Transport Service
GLOBAL
RESPONSIVE
RAPID
Airlifts 15,358 combat troops.
Plus 1,000,000 pounds of battle equipment.
Within 70 hours.
UNITED STATES to EUROPE.
For U. S. ARMY and TACTICAL AIR COMMAND.
Demonstrates massive reinforcement of NATO with U. S. STRIKE COMMAND FORCES.

CHAPTER FOUR

"Big Lift"-15,000 to Europe in 2½ Days

THUNDERING OVER the long runway near Frankfurt, Germany, the four jet engines of the MATS C-135 Stratolifter throttled down. The giant sweptwing aircraft swung lower, its wheels touched, rolled along, and finally it slowed to a stop. U.S. airmen wheeled passenger steps bearing the words "Rhein-Main" up to the door.

First out, clad in battle dress, was the major general commanding the "Hell on Wheels" 2nd Armored Division. Following the general, helmeted and carrying their side arms and personal gear, came the division headquarters staff.

That same day, at one minute after midnight on October 22, 1963 – a scant 10½ hours before – this same Boeing C-135 took off from Bergstrom Air Force Base in Texas to begin the massive airlift of the entire 2nd Armored Division. Now, every hour for the first twenty-four hours of "Big Lift," a MATS jet transport aircraft would be winging its way over the Atlantic, flying the 5,600 miles to off-load its cargo of American troops in Europe.

Doing their part in the lift and making the same journey as well were the MATS propeller-driven air transports. In all, during the entire 2½-day operation, a participating MATS plane would be landing or taking off on the average of once every six minutes. In this phenomenally short time, a total of 15,358 officers and men of the "Hell on Wheels" Division, Army support troops, Tactical Air Force ground personnel, and more than a million pounds of battle equipment were delivered to some eight air bases in France and Germany.

Remarkable as the 2½-day period seems for airlifting so many men and so much equipment, Big Lift was actually accomplished during peacetime without real pressure. But when the chips are down, MATS can be relied upon to break all records. MATS commander

Gen. Joe W. Kelly put it this way: "If we went into full swing on a wartime basis we could do it in 40 hours." That's little more than a day and a half.

In what was the largest transatlantic Army-Air Force deployment ever made by air, the U.S. Department of Defense exercise Big Lift put a complete Army division and elements of a Tactical Air Command strike force across the ocean in one mammoth operation. Four squadrons of tactical fighter and reconnaissance aircraft of the Composite Air Strike Force (CASF) accompanied the MATS transports making the crossing "under their own steam." However, the major part of the cargo carried by MATS — 680,000 pounds of it — was CASF equipment, and the total number of troops carried in MATS aircraft included close to 400 airmen.

Another distinction racked up by Big Lift was playing the part of a matchmaker for a wedding. In the words of the Secretary of Defense it was "the first exercise to link up a major U.S. based land force with combat material positioned overseas ready for pickup and use." The troops carried only their rifles, packs, and duffel bags from the states. The heavy equipment — tanks, artillery, vehicles, etc. — was assembled and waiting for them in staging areas in Europe. It was this joining of the men with their armor and "big guns" that newsmen on the spot called a "marriage."

Big Lift began with the onloading at two Army airfields and ten Air Force bases located in eight states of the South and southwestern United States. The tactical jet fighters and reconnaissance aircraft took off from Maine and Massachusetts.

In this exercise MATS employed different types of its transport aircraft — pure jet, jet propeller (or turboprop), and conventional propeller. In the hands of 355 MATS aircrews, with a strength of 3,000 men, they accomplished this unprecedented aerial delivery of troops and equipment in 234 missions.

Only 23 of the MATS planes were jet Stratolifters, able to carry 75 men each and make the trip, nonstop, in 10½ hours. Close to half of the 204 aircraft employed were Douglas C-124 Globemasters. This trusty piston engine transport carried 80 troops and cargo but took approximately 30¾ hours — three times as long as the jet carrier. Included in the C-124's travel time were two refueling stops at Bermuda and the Azores or at Newfoundland and England.

The other participants in Big Lift were 18 Douglas C-133 Cargomasters each lifting 10 troops and cargo, over the northern route, in

21 hours; 35 Douglas C-118 Liftmasters with a capacity of 57 troops each; and 30 Lockheed C-130E Hercules that carried 60 troops and cargo. The C-118's made the journey in about 21½ hours and the C-130E's did it in approximately 1½ hours less time. Both aircraft followed either the northern or southern routes depending upon scheduling and weather. The MATS transports were exclusive of the 116 tactical jet fighters recon aircraft and MATS Technical Service planes that also took part in Big Lift.

The 500-mph C-135's made two or three trips each within the 2½-day period, while their conventional propeller- and turboprop-driven sister ships completed only one mission apiece.

What was Big Lift like for the "passengers" — the troops of the 2nd Armored Division? A typical flight went something like this:

Early in the morning of October 22, 72 soldiers boarded air-conditioned buses at their home base in Fort Hood, Texas, and were driven to Bergstrom Air Force Base. Aboard their Stratolifter they were greeted by a MATS Flight Traffic Specialist. She wore the light-blue blouse and blue slacks of the WAF uniform. On behalf of the crew she wished the soldiers a pleasant journey.

By this time the men were comfortably seated in reclining chairs. Just as in regular commercial overwater flights, they were instructed in the use of the "Mae West" life preserver and the oxygen mask. The "No smoking" and "Fasten seat belt" signs were also indicated.

Once aloft, the soldiers had the freedom of the plane and wandered at will up and down the aisle visiting with their buddies. Some read or played cards, others slept, and all took advantage of the coffee and snacks readily available to them. The fight attendant also served in-flight rations.

Again, as on a regular airliner, they were briefed frequently over the loudspeaker. One of the three pilots aboard would tell them the altitude at which they were flying, their location, the weather outside, and the ETA (estimated time of arrival).

As soon as they disembarked at the Rhein-Main air base they were fed at a mess hall on the field. Following "chow" they picked up their two duffel bags that had been off-loaded for them while they ate. Then they mounted trucks and buses and were taken 60 miles to their bivouac area. Here they set up the shelter halves they had carried in their packs, and slept through the cold German night. Barely ten hours before, the men had left Texas in 80° temperature, warm enough for swimming. But for the soldiers it was an adventure — a new experience for most of them. The following morning they would be joined up with their equipment that had been pre-positioned awaiting their arrival.

Big Lift was a striking illustration of the United States' capability for rapid reinforcement of NATO forces, or of our own or Allied troops anywhere in the world. The Secretary of Defense indicated that the operation demonstrated "a new magnitude of U.S. military responsiveness." And the Supreme Allied Commander of NATO forces was certain that the capabilities presented by Big Lift "have been clearly noted by potential aggressors."

In effect, this massive exercise was the direct lineal descendant of the World War II "Hump" operations, "Vittles" — the relief of Berlin — and the numerous other MATS global airlifts. Indeed it was the end product, in experience and equipment, of these other historical missions that enable MATS to place an "air bridge" spanning oceans and continents into operation, virtually at will.

Considering the fact that approximately half of its strategic transport aircraft and 355 of its aircrews were engaged in Big Lift, MATS emphasizes the fact that "any emergency or crisis" could have been met during the maneuver. It did not strain their capabilities. In addition, the whole operation was carried on without requisitioning extra supplies or parts. On their return trips, the planes carried troops being rotated to the states and the customary MATS passengers and cargo. As they completed their part in the exercise, the aircraft were fitted back into the regular MATS routine.

As in all MATS operations, its component Technical Services played a part. Vital weather reports were provided by the Air Weather Service. The Air Rescue Service established overwater emergency "rescue orbits," which fortunately were not needed since Big Lift went off without a hitch. And the Air Photographic and Charting Service photographically "covered" the entire operation for later study and for the historical record.

Three months later, on January 30, 1964, MATS duplicated the feat — on the other side of the world — by airlifting the Hawaiian-based 25th Infantry Division to Okinawa. This was exercise "Quick Release."

Although exercises Big Lift and Quick Release marked a milestone in air transport history — the first time that any nation had made such dramatic airlifts of large numbers of men and supplies over such long distances in so short a time — it is really only the beginning. Shortly MATS will have its new C-141 Starlifter jets custom built for MATS global logistical operations. Mounting four powerful turbofan engines, the C-141 is a highly advanced model of its sister C-130 Hercules. These modern, high-speed "C-jets" will greatly increase MATS' capabilities and make possible even more dramatic airlifts.

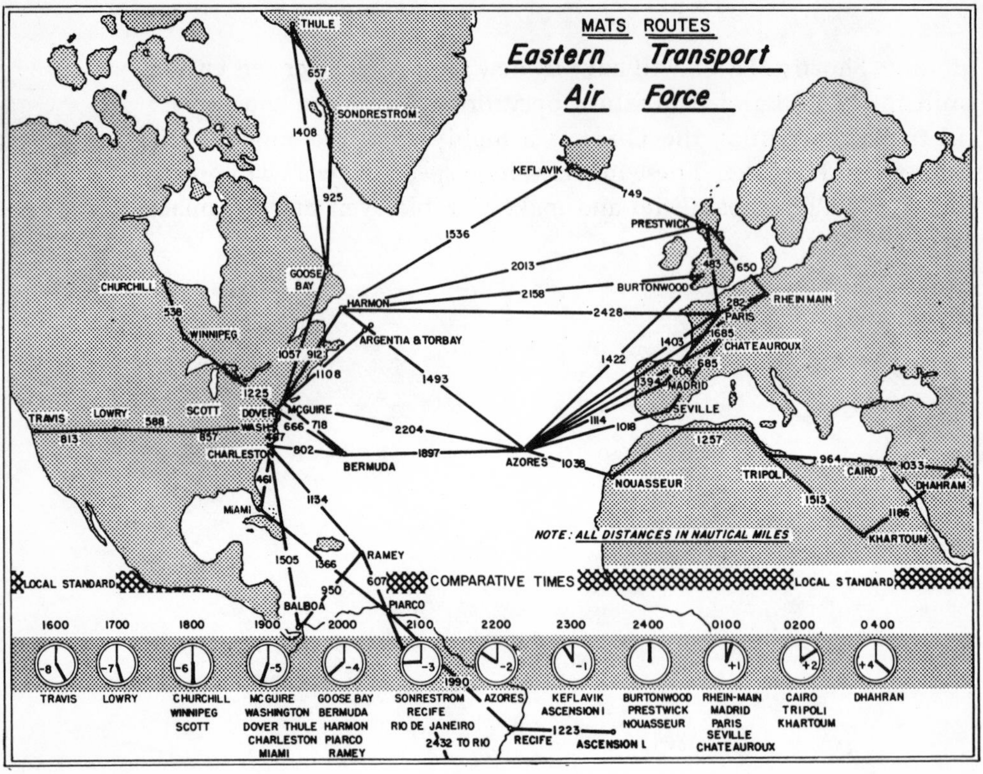
MATS ROUTES
Eastern Transport Air Force
THULE
657
1408
SONDRESTROM
925
KEFLAVIK
749
1536
PRESTWICK
GOOSE BAY
2013
483
650
CHURCHILL
BURTONWOOD
HARMON
2158
RHEIN MAIN
538
282
2428
PARIS
WINNIPEG
ARGENTIA & TORBAY
1685
1403
CHATEAUROUX
1057
912
1108
1493
1422
606
685
1394
MADRID
1225
TRAVIS
LOWRY
SCOTT
DOVER
MCGUIRE
SEVILLE
588
WASH
666
718
2204
1114
1018
813
857
447
CHARLESTON
802
BERMUDA
1897
AZORES
1038
1257
NOUASSEUR
TRIPOLI
964
CAIRO
1033
DHAHRAM
461
1134
1513
MIAMI
1186
KHARTOUM
NOTE: ALL DISTANCES IN NAUTICAL MILES
RAMEY
1505
1366
607
LOCAL STANDARD
COMPARATIVE TIMES
LOCAL STANDARD
950
BALBOA
PIARCO
1600
1700
1800
1900
2000
2100
2200
2300
2400
0100
0200
0400
-8
-7
-6
-5
-4
-3
-2
-1
+1
+2
+4
1990
TRAVIS
LOWRY
CHURCHILL
WINNIPEG
SCOTT
MC GUIRE
WASHINGTON
DOVER THULE
CHARLESTON
MIAMI
GOOSE BAY
BERMUDA
HARMON
PIARCO
RAMEY
SONRESTROM
RECIFE
RIO DE JANEIRO
AZORES
KEFLAVIK
ASCENSION I
BURTONWOOD
PRESTWICK
NOUASSEUR
RHEIN-MAIN
MADRID
PARIS
SEVILLE
CHATEAUROUX
CAIRO
TRIPOLI
KHARTOUM
DHAHRAN
RECIFE
1223
ASCENSION I.
2432 TO RIO

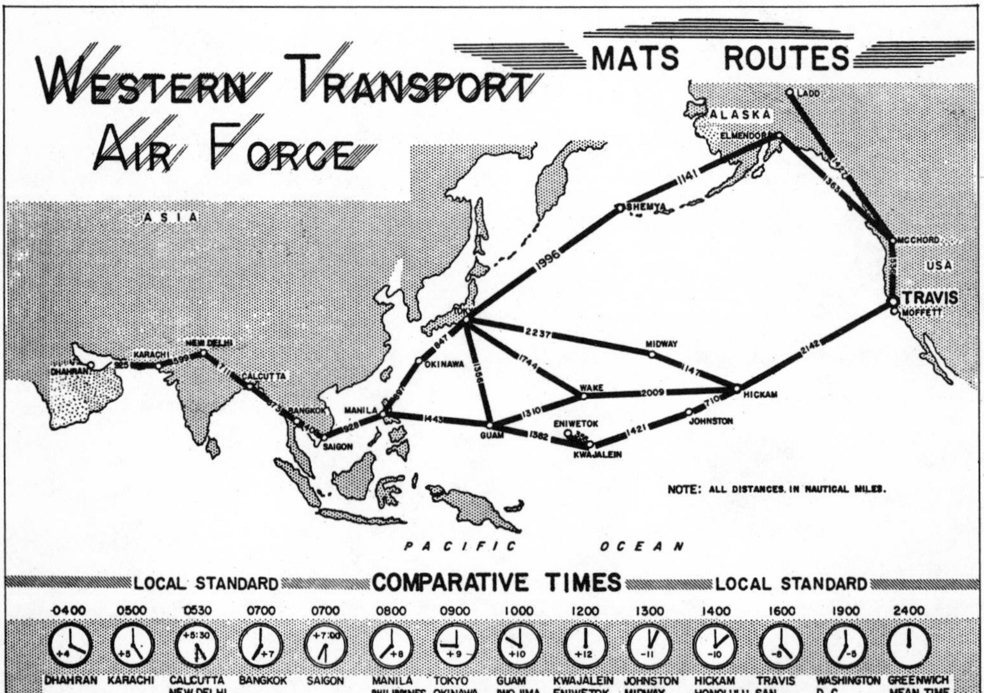
MATS ROUTES
WESTERN TRANSPORT AIR FORCE
LADD
ALASKA
ELMENDORF
1141
SHEMYA
1477
1363
MCCHORD
USA
1996
TRAVIS
MOFFETT
ASIA
2237
MIDWAY
2142
NEW DELHI
KARACHI
925
599
DHAHRAN
CALCUTTA
847
OKINAWA
1744
1147
1560
WAKE
2009
HICKAM
710
BANGKOK
MANILA
1310
JOHNSTON
1443
ENIWETOK
1421
SAIGON
928
GUAM
1382
KWAJALEIN
NOTE: ALL DISTANCES IN NAUTICAL MILES.
PACIFIC OCEAN
LOCAL STANDARD
COMPARATIVE TIMES
LOCAL STANDARD
0400
0500
0530
0700
0700
0800
0900
1000
1200
1300
1400
1600
1900
2400
+4
+5
+5:30
+7
+7:00
+8
+9
+10
+12
-11
-10
-8
-5
DHAHRAN
KARACHI
CALCUTTA
NEW DELHI
BANGKOK
SAIGON
MANILA
PHILIPPINES
TOKYO
OKINAWA
FORMOSA
GUAM
IWOJIMA
KWAJALEIN
ENIWETOK
WAKE
JOHNSTON
MIDWAY
INT. DATELINE
HICKAM
HONOLULU
TRAVIS
SAN FRANCISCO
WASHINGTON
D. C.
GREENWICH
MEAN TIME

CHAPTER FIVE

EASTAF, WESTAF, All Around the World

Scheduled Global Airlift

As a MATS Transport pilot, I recognize my obligations in the following Code:

- *To the United States Armed Forces, who trust that I am professionally qualified for the tasks expected of me.*
- *To the passengers who trust their lives and safety to my skill and judgment.*
- *To my fellow pilots, who depend upon me to follow established good practices.*
- *To my crew members, who expect me to exercise my best judgment and leadership.*
- *To my coworkers, who constantly are striving for greater achievements in the Military Air Transport Service.*
- *To my organization which entrusts me, in the conduct of my flights, with moral and economic responsibilities.*
- *To discharge these responsibilities, I will at all times observe the highest standards as an officer of the U.S. Air Force (and Navy), and as a professional transport pilot.*
- *I will never knowingly jeopardize the safety of a flight by undertaking a risk to satisfy personal desires, nor will I fly when my mental and physical condition might lead to additional risks.*
- *I will use all means at my disposal to assure the safety of every flight.*

- *I will aggressively maintain my proficiency as a pilot and keep abreast of aviation developments so that my judgment, which largely depends on such knowledge, may be of the highest order.*
- *I will conduct myself, both on duty and off, to reflect credit upon myself, my uniform and my country.*
- *I will constantly strive to keep my standards high.*
- *I pledge adherence to these principles so that I may contribute my part to a safer and more efficient Military Air Transport Service and advance the diginity of my profession.*

THE *kamaainas* (residents) who were picking pineapples in the fields near Honolulu paused in their work to look up at the great silver plane circling to land at Hickam Air Force Base. It was a MATS transport on its way in from Travis Air Force Base, California, bound for Tachikawa Air Base near Tokyo.

Simultaneously, similar scenes were being repeated over the rice paddies of Taiwan; the streets of Paris, France; Frankfurt, Germany; Charleston, South Carolina; and numerous other spots across Europe, Africa, the middle East, Asia, and in fact all around the globe.

At McGuire Air Force Base near Trenton, New Jersey, it was a quarter to four on a sticky, hot afternoon in August. Led by a sergeant clad in Air Force blue, a procession of some sixty-eight persons left the giant passenger terminal. They followed the Traffic Clerk through the gate, walking toward the military C-118 Liftmaster. The four-engine, silver, white, and orange aircraft, military version of the Douglas DC-6B, stood glistening on the field before them.

Among the passengers were airmen, soldiers, sailors, as well as Army, Navy, and Air Force officers. In addition, there were many children and wives — dependents of military personnel. Other civilians included teachers, librarians, secretaries, and more employees of the Department of Defense, State Department, and other government agencies.

Two Air Force Flight Attendants directed the passengers to their seats. Although the C-118 resembles the DC-6B in practically every other way, the military model of the Liftmaster has the seats facing to the rear. There is a row of double seats on one side of the aircraft and a row of three seats on the other side. An aisle separates the two rows of seats.

On this particular flight, a sergeant, in an Army green uniform, sat on the aisle. His wife was next to the window and their three-year-old daughter sat between them. The other sixty-five passengers filled the remaining seats.

Once the doors were secured the flight attendants briefed the passengers on routine overwater flight procedure. They demonstrated the use of the "Mae West," that yellow-colored, inflatable life jacket that the passengers would have to use in the event engine trouble or other emergencies forced the pilot to "ditch" in the Atlantic Ocean.

The young attendant, wearing the two stripes of an Airman 2nd Class on her sleeves, even brought over a baby Mae West and explained its use to the Army sergeant and his wife, who was now holding the child on her lap.

From the time that the briefing had begun, the four engines started to turn over — first the two on the right, then the ones on the left. The pilot was warming them up and getting them into synchronization. Soon the big plane began taxiing down the field. In a few moments the pilot got the OK from the control tower. He opened up the throttle, the motors roared, and the huge transport surged forward. Faster and faster it hurtled down the runway, then lifted gracefully into the air. Peering from the windows, the passengers could see houses and cars rapidly becoming smaller as the Liftmaster climbed toward the clouds. In a short while the land disappeared beneath them and they were over the Atlantic.

"Good evening," came the voice over the aircraft's public-address system. "This is Major Berger speaking. Welcome aboard MATS flight 407 from McGuire Air Force Base to the Royal Air Force Station at Mildenhall, England. We have just flown over Long Island. In four hours we will make a refueling stop at Harmon, Newfoundland. As soon as we reach the cruising altitude of 17,000 feet the flight attendants will distribute the in-flight lunches."

"For some reason," commented a Marine colonel, obviously a veteran of many MATS flights, "they always seem to call them 'lunches' whether its four o'clock in the morning or suppertime."

". . . and that bit about the refueling stop in four hours," said a private first class to his buddy across the aisle, "they make it to Rhein-Main in Germany nonstop in those new jet C-135's in far less time than it takes us to fly to England."

"I know!" replied his companion. "One of the guys in my outfit said that it's the same as a Boeing 707 and they made the flight to Germany in less than ten hours."

"Man, that's really moving!"

And so the flight continued. . . .

What is the actual makeup of this worldwide system that functions so smoothly?

For the first ten years of its existence MATS operated with three major air transport divisions that physically circled the globe. These were the Atlantic, Pacific, and Continental Divisions.

In 1958, the year of its tenth anniversary, MATS underwent a reorganization. What previously had been called the Atlantic Division became EASTAF, or Eastern Transport Air Force. Concurrently, WESTAF or Western Transport Air Force replaced the Pacific Division. Except for the domestic medical aerial evacuation routes traveled by MATS, there is no counterpart for the old Continental Division which provided aerial transportation over the United States coast to coast, to Alaska, Panama, Puerto Rico, and South America.

MATS, being principally an over-ocean transport operator, this change was strictly in keeping with its mission.

EASTAF and WESTAF are responsible for the channel traffic — the principal military air routes across the Atlantic and Pacific oceans. This global airlift operation is its reason for being and, to accomplish it, one-half of MATS personnel are assigned to the task.

Indeed, it is the very lifeblood of the Military Air Transport Service and, for that matter, of the United States itself. The headquarters at EASTAF and WESTAF handle the regular MATS scheduled flights that span the world, as well as the humanitarian and strategic airlifts that arise from time to time. And, while conducting these operations which are, strictly speaking, training missions, MATS air transport crews are flying the routes. In addition, the ground personnel are doing the jobs they would be doing in any national emergency or international crisis.

The major continental United States passenger aerial ports of embarkation or debarkation are Travis Air Force Base in California, and McGuire Air Force Base. Travis serves WESTAF as headquarters and dispatches transport aircraft over the Pacific routes, while McGuire, headquarters of EASTAF, processes aircraft to Europe,

Africa, and return. Two other MATS aerial ports are EASTAF's Charleston Air Force Base, in South Carolina, servicing United States obligations in South America and the Caribbean and providing an alternate route to Europe and Africa; and McChord Air Force Base, in the state of Washington, which handles the MATS traffic to and from Alaska.

All of these bases process cargo as well as passengers. In fact, MATS global air transport aircraft are geared for cargo with a convertibility feature which allows for passengers and aeromedical evacuation. In addition, EASTAF has Dover Air Force Base, in Delaware, which handles cargo traffic exclusively to Europe; and Hunter Air Force Base, in Georgia, which houses an EASTAF Troop Carrier Wing.

In effect, EASTAF and WESTAF have divided the globe between them. With some 330 airlift aircraft, EASTAF flies the military air routes north to Greenland and Iceland. It supports the United States space program with its regular flights to Brazil and Ascension Island in the South Atlantic, and it flies east to Europe, Africa, and the Near East, halfway around the world to just east of Calcutta, India.

On the other side of the earth, WESTAF operates over the Pacific with about 265 airlift aircraft. Its routes extend north to Alaska, south to the island bases in the Pacific, and west to Japan and across Asia to meet EASTAF east of Calcutta.

The final link in the MATS routes girdling the globe are the domestic aeromedical evacuation routes across the United States. These evacuation flights are the responsibility of the 1405th Aeromedical Transport Wing, Scott Air Force Base, Ill.

In order to get a better idea of the scope of this vast air transport operation, here is a breakdown of the EASTAF network. The Eastern Transport Air Force consists of one air division and seven wings of aircraft. Four of these (three Air Force and one Navy) and one Troop Carrier Wing are based in the United States at McGuire, Dover, Charleston, and Hunter fields. The remaining two wings and the air division provide overseas en route and logistical support. The wings are located at Bermuda, and the Azores, and the air division at Châteauroux, France. Additional smaller support units are located in Iceland, Newfoundland, Greenland, Labrador, England, Scotland, Germany, Spain, Morocco, Tripoli, Egypt, Saudi Arabia, Puerto Rico, Panama, Brazil, and Cape Kennedy.

WESTAF operates in similar fashion with its overseas logistical and support wings strung out across the Pacific and Asia. One

WESTAF wing is stationed at Hickam Air Force Base, in Hawaii, and another at Tachikawa, outside of Tokyo.

No story of MATS or of its two principal operating elements, EASTAF and WESTAF, would be complete without mention of the 1707th Air Transport Wing. Housed at Tinker Air Force Base, Oklahoma, the 1707th is the MATS advanced training unit for flight crews and ground personnel.

Before a pilot, navigator, or mechanic is assigned to an operational unit with responsibility for passengers, he must go through the training program at Tinker. This is a rigid MATS requirement, regardless of how experienced a pilot may be – even if he has flown commercial airliners or transport aircraft in other branches of the service.

The Special Air Missions (SAM) or 1254th Air Transport Wing is also considered part of the MATS global airlift force. It operates out of the Washington, D.C., area and provides nonscheduled special air transport for the President, high government officers, and other VIP's. The story of the 1254th is covered in detail in a later chapter of this book.

In 1958, the year following MATS' big reorganization, the outward similarity between it and the United States commercial airlines was pronounced. Passengers traveled free on MATS aircraft. This feature should have made it the most popular air carrier anywhere, except for the fact that it had a very restricted and exclusive clientele. Upon reorganization, MATS went into an Industrial Funding Program. MATS' "customers" – the Army, Navy, and Air Force – began paying for required airlift services, as needed, on a cost basis.

Although all of the participants are part of the United States government and the new cost basis may look like "taking from one pocket to put into the other," Industrial Funding really served to give MATS a great deal of flexibility. It provided the means by which the service could buy as much commercial overseas air transportation as needed by the other branches of the government. The only limitation on this capability is the amount of money the Army, Navy, and Air Force can spend for airlift.

How does all of this fit into the total picture? And, specifically, what were the preliminary preparations that took place before the Army sergeant, his wife, and his infant daughter boarded the MATS C-118 at McGuire Air Force Base? Well, one thing is certain. He didn't call up the day before and make a reservation (although in emergencies and special cases there is enough flexibility in the MATS process so that this could be done).

Normally, the sergeant would have channeled his reservation through a system known as the Requirements and Allocations Cycle. Three months before this, a group of Army officers would have met and calculated the need for that period. They also would have estimated the cost since the Army would have to pay for the airlift under the Industrial Funding Program. These requirements would then have been forwarded to MATS Headquarters at Scott Air Force Base in Illinois at least 80 days before lift. Here would be determined the amount of commercial space needed to augment MATS' own overwater capabilities. Since the same procedure is also followed by the Air Force and the Navy, 52 days in advance of flight time, MATS Headquarters made space allocations to the three services. These assignments were then forwarded to EASTAF and WESTAF 49 days prior to departure. The two transport air forces then published their Monthly Operations Bulletin 40 days before the flight.

The Army, once it had been notified of its space assignments, was then able to issue orders to the sergeant calling for assignment to the office of the U.S. Military Attaché at the Embassy in London. Since the orders called for a permanent change of station he was authorized to bring his family. The sergeant also had time to take care of personal business, arrange for transportation to Trenton, New Jersey, and McGuire Air Force Base, and "to clear the post" (that is, turn in any organizational equipment he might have had, such as sheets, blankets, etc.).

Upon his arrival at McGuire, the sergeant reported to the Air Traffic Coordinating Officer (ATCO). Each of the services has its own ATCO at the aerial ports of embarkation, and these officers represent their own branch of the service and act as liaison with MATS.

The Army ATCO then checked the sergeant's orders and confirmed his space aboard MATS flight 407. From here on the procedure was similar to that followed by the commercial airlines.

This process is a continuing one that accounts for the assignment of overseas airlift space on MATS and contract aircraft every day of the year. And to make certain that the system is operating fairly and efficiently, the Joint Military Transportation Committee regularly reviews and monitors it.

That is how the sergeant and his family managed to be on board the Liftmaster on their way to his new assignment in London.

And that is how MATS and its major operating air transport forces, EASTAF and WESTAF, carry virtually countless numbers of corporals, sergeants, lieutenants, captains, colonels, generals, and privates as well, to their various assignments around the world.

MATS and Bell-Bottom Trousers–The Naval Air Transport Service

Although MATS is a major command of the Air Force, on a par with the Strategic Air Command, Tactical Air Command, and the Air Defense Command, bell-bottom trousers happen to be the uniform of some MATS crews. In fact, the U.S. Navy has been a part of MATS ever since the command came into existence in 1948. At that time the Naval Air Transport Service (NATS) was combined with the Air Force's Air Transport Command (ATC).

The Navy has flown alongside the Air Force since the merger of the two air transport services. Historically, Navy aircrews have participated in practically every major MATS airlift operation. They have flown in the Berlin Airlift, Korean War, Suez, Lebanon, Vietnam, Cuba, and other lifts.

In the Korean War alone, MATS Navy squadrons airlifted 17,000 battle casualties. This figure represents 25 per cent of the total sick and wounded aeromedically evacuated from Korea.

In addition, MATS Navy air personnel also took part in the training exercises Big Slam/Puerto Pine, Long Pass, Long Thrust, and others. And from the start of "Operation Deep Freeze" in the Antarctic, MATS Navy air transport has actively furnished support.

In its original organization, MATS was set up in three divisions – Atlantic, Pacific, and Continental. A rear admiral commanded the Pacific Division and another rear admiral served as the MATS vice commander. Under the reorganization that took place ten years later, the Continental Division was eliminated, EASTAF replaced the Atlantic Division, and WESTAF took the place of the Pacific Division. Air Force major generals were put in command of both of the transport air forces; however, senior naval officers were also assigned to their staffs and to MATS headquarters.

Most of the Navy people assigned to MATS – some 2,900 of them

—are engaged in global airlift operations. Although they constitute only 5 per cent of the MATS strategic airlift force, Navy pilots and crews account for 18 per cent of the air transport units' total flying hours.

EASTAF and WESTAF share fairly equally in the naval flying squadrons allotted to MATS. VR-3, an air transport squadron, is assigned to McGuire Air Force Base and VR-22, a composite, self-supporting squadron, is based at the Naval Air Transport Station in Norfolk, Virginia. Together they constitute EASTAF's Naval Air Transport Wing, Atlantic.

On the West Coast, Naval Air Transport Wing, Pacific, consists of Air Transport Squadron VR-7 and Maintenance Squadron VR-8 based at the Naval Air Station, Moffett Field, California. A detachment of VR-7 is also stationed at Tachikawa Air Base in Japan.

Navy crews all fly the C-130E Hercules, except for the detachment in Japan which flies C-121's.

The MATS Navy crews fly over scheduled MATS routes to Newfoundland, Iceland, Scotland, Germany, Italy, Puerto Rico, and Africa. Over the Pacific, the MATS Navy crews wing their way to Hawaii, Wake Island, Guam, the Philippines, Alaska, Japan, Korea, Bangkok, Saigon, and other stops in the Far East.

Strength in Reserve-CRAF, Air Force Reserve, and Air National Guard

In addition to the overseas airlifting that MATS can purchase from commercial airlines in the event of war, they can count on some 242 aircraft with a global airlift capability. Within forty-eight hours after the declaration of a national emergency, MATS would be augmented by this reserve air fleet provided by more than twenty United States commercial airlines.

This program, which has been in effect since 1951, is known as the Civil Reserve Air Fleet or CRAF. It enables MATS to increase its wartime global airlift for a very small portion of the cost it would otherwise have had to pay to maintain so many aircraft on a full-time basis. In this way, the airlines have the use of the air transports (which they own) and maintain them, while at the same time they are available to MATS in time of need.

In its arrangements with the participating carriers, MATS has available to it the aforementioned aircraft that have been earmarked for its use "when the chips are down." These are suitable four-engine cargo and passenger aircraft of the United States commercial airlines which have an "overwater" capability. To insure that all CRAF aircraft can deliver this essential long-range performance, MATS instituted a modification program for the installation of wiring and brackets to receive the necessary communications and navigation equipment. They have also maintained a modernization program.

However, CRAF is only a part of MATS' "strength in reserve." There is yet another boost available to it in time of war or other national emergency!

This, MATS' "ace in the hole," is a large number of air reserve forces. Composed of civilians, including both veterans and newcomers, these Air Force reservists and Air National Guardsmen train one weekend a month and two weeks each summer to maintain their MATS military proficiency. They total 210 units, 34,000 personnel, 233 aircraft, and are steadily expanding their numbers.

CHAPTER SIX

Special Air Missions (SAM)

PEERING FROM his window, the President of the United States could make out the White House, the Capitol Building, the Pentagon, the Lincoln Memorial, and other familiar Washington landmarks as his big four-engine jet transport swung around the nation's capital for a landing at Andrews Air Force Base.

The President had been in the careful hands and under the watchful eyes of MATS' Special Air Missions, fondly called "SAM," and officially known as the 1254th Air Transport Wing, Special Missions. It is this elite group that flies the Presidential aircraft – the four VC-137A jet transports – modified versions of the commercial airlines' Boeing 707 (which had themselves been developed from the Air Force jet KC-135 Stratotanker).

The President's personal aircraft is generally known as "US No. 1" or "Air Force No. 1." It was on Air Force 1 that Lyndon B. Johnson was sworn into office following the assassination of President Kennedy on November 22, 1963, in Dallas, Texas.

In the past, the 1254th was also the custodian of former personal Presidential aircraft such as President Eisenhower's VC-121 Constellation, the *Columbine*, and President Truman's *Independence*, successors to President Franklin D. Roosevelt's famous *Sacred Cow*. Though they are often a world away, these carefully picked crew members are practically members of the White House staff.

If SAM were a small airline, its passenger manifest would be the most exclusive in the world – these are the VIP's (Very Important Persons) who top any "Who's Who." Numbered among SAM's guests have been the chiefs of state and heads of government of many countries throughout the world. These have included kings and queens, princes, presidents, prime ministers, not to speak of the President of the United States, the Vice-President, the Secretary of

State, and other top government cabinet and military officers.

The Soviet Union's Nikita Khrushchev was a Special Air Missions passenger on his tour of the United States in the fall of 1959. A few months prior to that, SAM had taken Vice-President Richard Nixon to Moscow and Warsaw. They were also constantly flying that well-traveled Secretary of State, John Foster Dulles, to every corner of the globe. This activity has even been stepped up with the succeeding Presidents and Secretaries of State as the world grows smaller and U.S. international commitments and obligations grow larger.

The motto of the Special Air Missions Group is *"Experto Crede* — Trust One With Experience." And experience is their watchword. These are all handpicked men. Despite the fact that every pilot selected for SAM is a fully qualified MATS aircraft commander, thoroughly familiar with overwater, instrument, and night flying, he still spends close to a year flying as a copilot in the 1254th. The minimum qualification for four-engine pilots is 4,000 flying hours, with at least 1,000 of them in transport aircraft. Twin-engine pilots must have at least 3,000 hours. If these standards seem rigid, they are even more stringent for the "cream of the crop" — the nine jet pilots who fly the four VC-137's. On their shoulders rests the responsibility for the President of the United States and other chiefs of state — not to mention a $5,500,000 four-jet transport aircraft loaded with specialized equipment.

This same high selection standard also goes for the rest of the flying crew, household personnel, and ground crew. From the aircraft commander down, they must all be "diplomats" and intelligent representatives of the United States. On the President's aircraft, for example, in addition to the pilot, there is a copilot, navigator, two flight engineers, and a radio operator. Today, an airborne radio operator is unique among Air Force units, but since clear and ever present communication is vital to the President and other VIP's, the radio operator is a member of the crew on these SAM transport aircraft.

The signal equipment they use has up to 45,000 separate channels ensuring immediate contact through every radio and tower and control frequency on earth. It also connects by radio-telephone patch with every phone number in the world, and provides two-way teletype and cryptographic circuits that enable the President, or other important officials, to send and receive coded security classified messages.

Passengers boarding a MATS C-118 Liftmaster.

WAF Flight Attendant checks off each passenger against the manifest.

Aircraft of the MATS naval squadrons, along with their MATS Air Force counterparts, did an effective job of aeromedical evacuation during the Korean War. When they weren't carrying wounded, they were airlifting much needed supplies.

The *Columbine,* personal aircraft of President Eisenhower. This VIP Super Constellation was staffed and maintained by the MATS Special Air Missions Squadron.

One of the most versatile of the Air Rescue Service's equipment is the helicopter. In areas where it is impractical to land, it can hover over an injured soldier and pick him up by means of a sling attached to a 100-foot steel cable. The cable is powered by a special hydraulic-electric hoist.

Ready to jump into jungle, desert, mountains, or any place that an aircraft can't get, are the ARS Pararescuemen. Jumping in two-man teams, Pararescuemen are able to help the sick or wounded who cannot help themselves and get them back to safety.

When the pounding surf flooded an Army tug off Okinawa, an Air Rescue Service helicopter lifted the crew to safety.

Air rescuemen help one of the 32 survivors of a Northwest Airlines Strato-cruiser which crashed into Puget Sound. Within minutes of the emergency call, two ARS Albatrosses were on the scene.

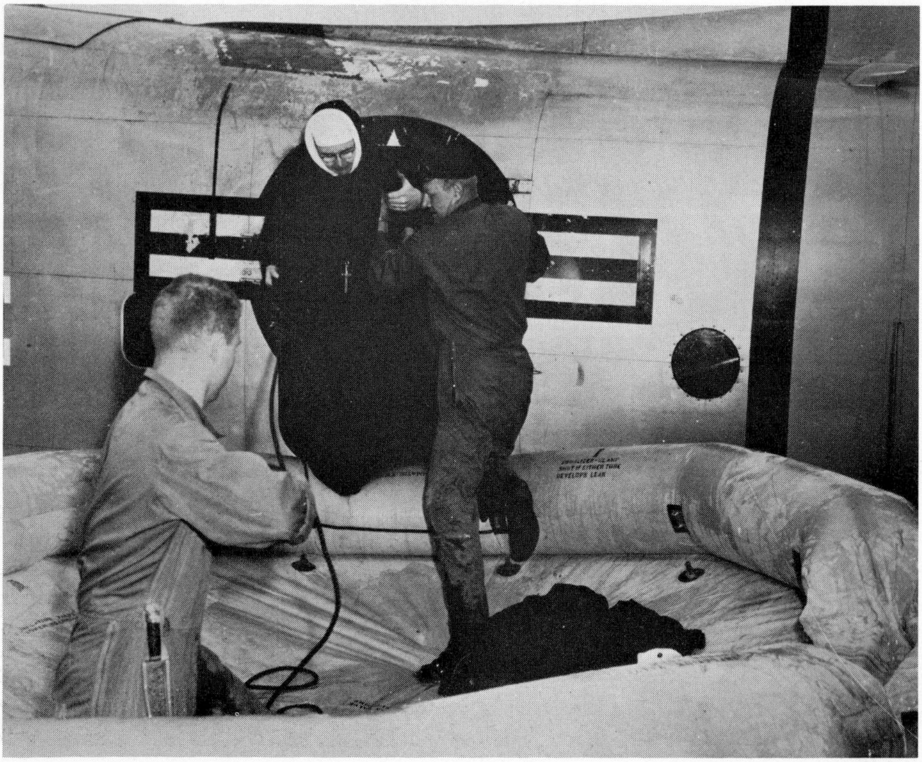

An AWS crew member about to replace a *dropsonde.* This instrument drops by parachute into the sea and sends back data on temperature, pressure, and humidity by radio to the aircraft.

An acetate overlay showing a 1000-millibar analysis of the northern hemisphere is being lifted off of the map. A 1000-millibar analysis is a sea-level chart showing high and low pressure systems.

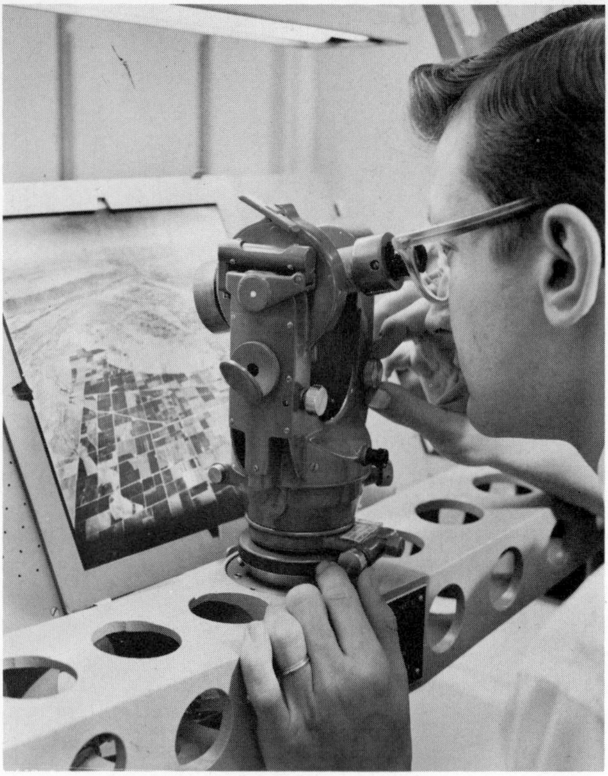

"Astrogeodesists" of the MATS Air Photographic and Charting Service using modern aerial photos and alidade can, with their knowledge of surveyors' mathematics, calculate more elevations in a day from a comfortable chair than the footsore surveyor can cover in two weeks.

"I will remember, that upon my disposition and spirit, will in large measure depend the morale of my patients. . . ."

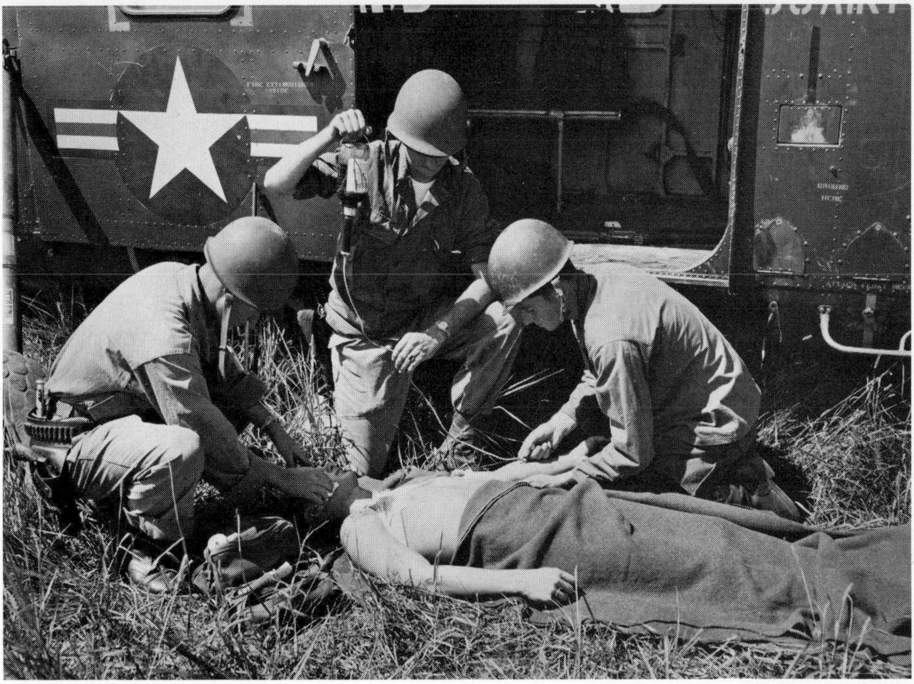

A wounded soldier being given whole blood on the battlefield of Korea before being flown by helicopter to a hospital beyond the lines.

Inside the "flying hospital ward," a Flight Nurse makes her rounds of the litter and ambulatory patients.

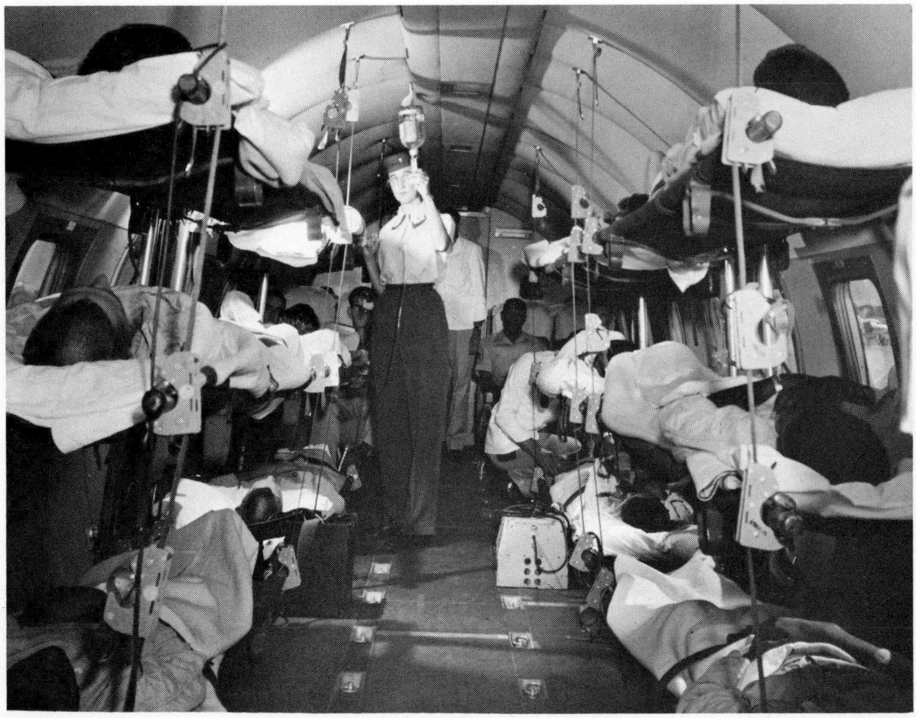

A MATS C-133 Cargomaster takes aboard a Thor IRBM bound for England. The C-133 can airlift any such outsize, high-priority cargo to any spot on the globe in a matter of hours.

Aeromedical Evacuation patients are usually members of our armed forces, the US government, their dependents, and military and government personnel of our allies. There are special cases, however. This little German boy, with an incurable heart condition, was carried by MATS from Rhein-Main in Frankfurt to McGuire Air Force Base, New Jersey, and on to the Mayo Clinic in Rochester, Minnesota through the regular MATS Aeromedical Evacuation System.

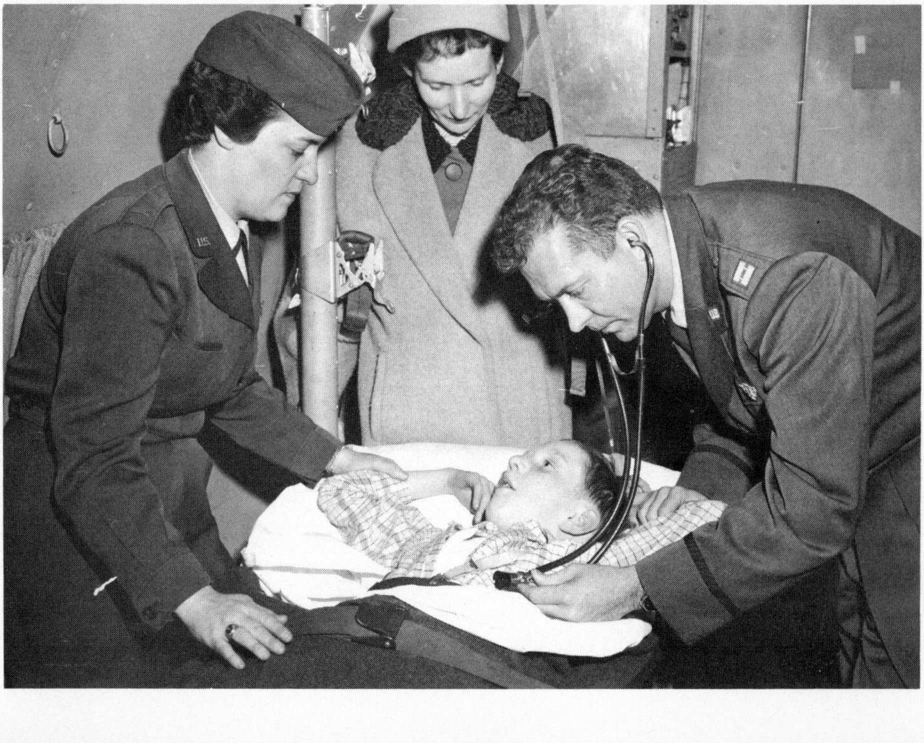

Another carefully selected member of the aircrew is the flight steward. He is the real diplomat of the organization. Because of the nature of his duties, he comes into direct contact with distinguished foreign passengers more often than any other member of the Special Air Missions Group. The flight steward is the "ambassador without portfolio," but — with tray. For the period of time that he spends with foreign dignitaries, he represents America.

The 1254th Air Transport Wing is the good right "arm" of United States diplomacy. For that very reason punctuality is of prime importance. SAM's passenger list being what it is, the crews know that they are busy officials meeting equally important people. Time is normally precious and short, and appointments very close; therefore, schedules are extremely tight — but MATS meets them. In fact, on one mission taking a high-level government official to more than thirty en route stops around the world, SAM was only off a scant half-minute!

An amazing thing about SAM's ability to meet these tight schedules is that often they are prepared a month in advance, with little knowledge of the weather prospects. The man who saves the day and makes it possible to meet these "impossible" schedules is the navigator. The pilots rely on their navigators to chart the best possible course using the most favorable winds. The navigators don't let them down. In fact, SAM aircraft commanders will assure anybody that "our navigators can't be beat." This is no idle boast.

In July, 1959, shortly after SAM had taken delivery of its first VC-137 jet transports, the 1254th Air Transport Wing flew Vice-President Nixon on a record-breaking nonstop New York-to-Moscow flight. The MATS' intercontinental jet streaked the 4,800 miles to the Soviet capital in 8 hours and 54 minutes. This was an average speed of about 545 miles an hour, bettering a Soviet record established less than two weeks before by an Aeroflot TU-114 turboprop transport aircraft.

But MATS, together with its component SAM, are continually establishing new world records. In May, 1963, the Presidential VC-137 set a nonstop Washington-to-Moscow record. The jet covered the 5,004 miles — a greater distance than the New York-to-Moscow run — in fifteen minutes less time.

Speed records and punctuality notwithstanding, SAM maintains an enviable safety record which is the safest in the nation — if not in the world.

To sum up, it has also been said that SAM stood for *S*afety, *A*irlift, and a *M*ethod of furthering the good will of the United States.

CHAPTER SEVEN

A Friend Indeed-Air Rescue Service

It is my duty, as a member of the Air Rescue Service, to save life and to aid the injured.

I will be prepared at all times to perform my assigned duties quickly and efficiently, placing these duties before personal desires and comforts.

These things I do that others may live.

Code of an Air Rescue Man

GLISTENING LIKE four silver specks in the Korean sky with the sun's rays shimmering on their bright aluminum skins, the flight of F-84's winged their way over the Communist lines. With rockets, bombs, and napalm slung under their wings, the Thunderjets streaked for their target.

The time was 1812 hours. A short while before, in the briefing room, the Operations Officer had indicated a concentration of supplies and equipment on the enemy's main supply route. This was at a point just south of the North Korean village of Hukkyo-ri. Now they were over it. At the flight leader's command they peeled off, in sequence, for the attack.

Down they went, guns blazing, bombs released, and then zoomed up again. In his turn Lt. Robert Bolton made his dive. Now he armed his rockets and zeroed in on a boxcar. With a *whoosh* his salvo rocketed toward the target. There was a thunderous roar and a geyser of red and yellow flame, and the boxcar, loaded with ammunition, blasted apart. Bolton could feel the explosion as he tore for the clouds. Suddenly, with a loud clunk, his engine flamed out!

While the destruction to the supply dump had been virtually complete, the Chinese Reds had not sat idly by. Several batteries of antiaircraft guns were busily throwing up a hail of lead at the fast-moving jets. A piece of shrapnel had struck Bolton's engine.

"Blue Leader, Blue Leader, this is Blue 3. I flamed out! I'm bailing out over that cultivated field surrounded by woods to the southeast, at coordinates 364298. Do you read me?"

Bolton's earphones crackled as he heard, "Roger! This is Blue Leader. I see it. We'll fly cover. Good luck! Out."

While Bolton was ejecting from his crippled plane and slowly drifting to earth, Blue Leader was radioing in the "Mayday" call for help and the map coordinates of the downed airman. The other two members of the flight were busy blasting anything that moved in the field and woods below.

Landing in the open field, Bolton twisted his left ankle. Hauling in his chute, he hobbled and crawled painfully through the sodden rice paddy, heading for the cover of the edge of the woods.

At the same time Air Rescue, which had already received the word, had "scrambled" a Sikorsky SH-19 helicopter. Aboard were the pilot Lt. Robert Stevens, copilot Lt. Mort Morrison, and Sgt. Ed Sinclair – a pararescueman, a skilled paratrooper, and medical aidman.

Speed was the watchword now! The sun was rapidly sinking below the horizon and the "choppers" were not equipped to operate in the dark. The downed flyer, too, knew that time was running out on him. He also knew that the jets, which consumed fuel at a rapid rate, had already overstayed their limit – and those Red soldiers were getting menacingly closer, despite the overhead cover.

Unknown to the injured airman, his jet flight was about to pull out. They had, however, contacted a flight of Mustangs that would take up the vigil. These F-51's were retreads from World War II. Being of the old type, piston engine, propeller-driven aircraft, they consumed less fuel and had longer staying power.

The last light of day was barely showing when the Rescue whirlybird arrived on the scene. Lieutenant Stevens knew he had little time left but he made a quick pass around the area. He knew he'd never make it if he let Sergeant Sinclair "jump in" to help Bolton, put him into the sling, haul the injured man up, and send the sling down again for the paramedic.

"Mustang Leader, Mustang Leader, this is Rescue. Do you read me? Over," he radioed.

Back came the reply, "This is Mustang Leader — we read you loud and clear — go ahead, Rescue."

"This is Rescue. If you can keep those hostiles occupied I'll go in and get our boy!"

"Roger, Wilco!" snapped the Mustang Leader. "Go get him, Rescue! Tallyho!"

As the F-51's wheeled into position in the rapidly darkening sky above, the Rescue helicopter hovered and set down on the rice field. Before the chopper had actually touched down, the hatch door was open and the paramedic, crouching low to avoid the whirling blades and the enemy fire, was on his way, the mud sucking at his boots.

Watching this "show" in his behalf, Bolton painfully called out, "Over here, over here!"

In a flash Sinclair was beside him. "Look, Lieutenant, we've got to get out of here on the double! I'll carry you piggyback to the chopper and then we'll take care of that foot."

The injured officer nodded his head in assent, and Sinclair shifted him onto his back. With Bolton's arms around his neck and his feet around his waist, the pararescueman made for the helicopter. Only now did they become aware of the racket being kicked up by the hail of bullets, tracers, and other explosives from the fire fight between the enemy infantrymen and our protective fighter planes.

As the Rescue pilot lifted his whirlybird from the unfriendly North Korean rice field his earphones crackled, "Good show, Rescue! Well done! I hope you're around if I ever end up down there."

Smiling, and with a sigh of relief, Stevens shot back, "You fighter boys aren't so bad yourselves!"

Relaxed and drinking a hot cup of coffee, the rescued pilot stretched out his left leg as Sergeant Sinclair carefully unwound the strip of parachute nylon Bolton had wrapped around his ankle.

"It's just a bad sprain," said the paramedic, with the authority of the professional that he was. "You'll be up there chasing MIG's again in a couple of days."

In the already darkened sky the Air Rescue Service helicopter, mission accomplished, droned its way back to base.

While the foregoing was a fictionalized account, the rescue of "Lieutenant Bolton" is nevertheless a typical one. However, it is by no means the most dangerous rescue made by ARS.

Like the night in June, 1951, when First Lt. John J. Najarian brought his Rescue amphibian down on the Taedong River — deep behind the enemy lines — to rescue a downed fighter pilot. It was too dark to send a helicopter and by all rights the amphib shouldn't have gone in either — particularly on this strange, dark river, containing who knew what kind of floating debris. But Najarian, true to the tradition of the Rescue pilot, did it. Without lights, and under withering enemy fire, he got his man out.

There is also the story of Capt. Dan Miller who three times braved the relentless fire of the enemy. Courageously he brought his chopper down on a narrow ridge to rescue six wounded and exposed *enemy* infantrymen trapped behind the lines.

Like many another fighter pilot, Capt. Joe McConnell, with more than fifteen enemy aircraft to his credit, was rescued to fly and fight again. Shot down by a Communist MIG, McConnell parachuted into the Yellow Sea. ARS Lts. Bob Sullivan and Don Crabb plucked him out of the "drink."

In the bloodletting and destruction that was the Korean War, ARS developed, polished, and refined its rescue techniques to the highest degree of reliability. By their speed and efficiency they were able to help reduce the mortality rate of the wounded to almost half that of World War II. In addition, Air Rescue saved the lives of 9,680 United Nations fighting men — more than 10 per cent of whom were rescued from behind the enemy lines. The record speaks for itself and shows why the ARS was the most decorated unit in the Korean conflict.

Moreover, like MATS, its parent unit, ARS has an enviable record of peacetime service to civilians. Also like MATS, ARS is a worldwide organization. With headquarters at Orlando Air Force Base in Florida, it has had squadrons strategically placed in the Philippines, Hawaii, Japan, Okinawa, Alaska, Newfoundland, Greenland, Labrador, Tripoli, French Morocco, Saudi Arabia, Germany, England, Scotland, the Azores, Iceland, and Bermuda. In the continental United States, there are ARS squadrons in the states of California, Washington, Nevada, Texas, Michigan, and Florida.

During the first ten years of its existence — from May, 1946, through May, 1956 — Air Rescue Service saved a confirmed total of 44,520 lives. For the most part, these acts of heroism were performed during peacetime, and a major portion of the rescued were civilians. ARS has been active in floods and other disasters and has received the acclaim of Queens Elizabeth of England and Juliana of the Netherlands. And expressions of gratitude have come from every corner of the free world.

The guiding angel who symbolizes the ARS has covered the globe well with her protecting hands and wings. Since its founding in 1946, MATS' Air Rescue Service has been on the alert 24 hours a day, 365 days a year — to answer distress calls from anyone, anywhere, anytime — "that others may live."

CHAPTER EIGHT

Hurricane Hunters-The Air Weather Service

THE MASSIVE silver B-50 Superfort flew gracefully through the air, its four powerful engines beating a steady rhythmic hum over the choppy ocean 1,500 feet below. Suddenly the big bomber was lifted and tossed about like a leaf — as though some unseen giant had stretched out his hand, snatched it in mid-flight, and flung it away!

This was no ordinary combat plane on a bombing mission. In fact, it happened to be peacetime and the aircraft was armed only with radar, dropsondes, Doppler navigator, and other technical weather instruments for gathering data on humidity, wind speed and direction, and location. This was a WB-50 — the "W" standing for Weather. It belonged to the MATS' Air Weather Service and now it was heading smack into a hurricane — on purpose.

And why not? Weren't they from the 53rd Weather Reconnaissance Squadron, the "Hurricane Hunters"? Wasn't their motto, *Pro Bono Publico* — "For the Good of the Public"?

"Here it comes," shouted the captain as he fought to hold the controls, then lifted the converted bomber to 10,000 feet, where the turbulence was considerably less. The rest of the ten-man crew braced themselves for the "big blow" and the severe buffeting that was bound to follow. Well trained in meteorology, these men knew what to expect — and they knew what they were there for.

Purposefully, these experienced weathermen set about their duties — tracking and reporting on the path and progress of the hurricane. They knew that there was little they could do to stop the forward drive of the raging storm, but every bit of advance knowledge and warning they could provide would help cut down the loss of lives and the damage to hundreds of millions of dollars' worth of property.

A short while before, this weather bomber had been alerted by the Joint (Air Force, Navy, and Weather Bureau) Hurricane Warning Center in Miami, Florida. Its mission: Find the center of the storm and determine its intensity and general movement.

Taking off from its home field at Kindley Air Force Base on the island of Bermuda, the big WB-50 was guided by its navigator to the general vicinity of the storm. Then with the help of the radar operator and the weather observer they located the "eye" of the hurricane.

Sitting up front in the nose of the weather plane was the man for whom the rest of the crew is working — the weather observer whose reports back to the Joint Hurricane Warning Center in Miami were the purpose of the entire mission. From the comparative safety of their perch, 10,000 feet up, the weather observer is able to obtain data from the lower altitudes by releasing dropsondes. This amazing device — a collection of sensing instruments dropped by parachute — transmits its findings, by radio, to the aircraft.

As the big plane fights its way through storm clouds and driving rain, so thick that the tips of the wings are obscured, the radar observer picks out the path of least resistance through the raging turbulence. His radarscope also shows the hurricane's eye.

A sharp right turn and suddenly the WB-50 finds itself in a quiet, dead calm, area! No clouds are here and the sun is shining brightly. Below, the water is peaceful and serene. On all sides a towering, vertical mass of clouds extend from the ocean to heights of 30,000 to 60,000 feet.

This is the "eye" of the hurricane — a true phenomenon of nature! But behind the peace and serenity of that clifflike wall of clouds is the raging tempest through which the plane has just passed. With hardly a thought that they will again have to face this roaring fury before they can return home, the weather crew continue with their assignments.

After the passing of some twelve to seventeen hours, the "Hurricane Hunters" will be back at base, having completed their mission.

As today's weather crews will tell you: "Hurricane tracking isn't what it used to be ten to fifteen years ago. We've learned a lot, and radar and the Doppler navigator have made the job a lot easier." In fact, the crews look forward to a hurricane mission as an adventuresome diversion from their routine weather reconnaissance tracks.

Like all of the other MATS components, the Air Weather Service is a worldwide network of weather stations and weather squadrons, providing round-the-clock weather information to our far-flung Army and Air Force. In wartime the commanding general of an Army Corps or Division must have the latest, most accurate weather forecasts in planning his battle strategy — and AWS furnishes it to him.

Manned by some 11,000 personnel, AWS uses the latest, most complex electronic and scientific machinery to speed meteorological information to its "customers." This advanced equipment includes: Tiros weather satellites, weather rockets, specialized radar, improved transmitters, and a new semiautomatic weather observing and forecasting system.

In addition to all of these modern innovations, the Air Weather Service still flies 35,000 miles on routine reconnaissance missions, over the polar regions and the oceans, every single day.

Working together with the Navy and the U.S. Weather Bureau, AWS also tracks tornadoes in continental United States and typhoons in the Pacific. It is interesting to note that the hurricane is to the Atlantic and Caribbean what the typhoon is to the Pacific. Even more interesting is the fact that our word for hurricane comes from the West Indian words *hurri can,* which means "big wind." Typhoon comes from the Chinese words *tai fung* which means the same thing.

All three — the hurricane, typhoon, and tornado — are indeed "ill winds that blow no good," destroying property worth billions of dollars and costing countless lives. The MATS' Air Weather Service defies these cyclonic storms in order to save Air Force lives and equipment, the lives and property of American citizens, and of many other people all over the world.

CHAPTER NINE

Astrogeodesists-Air Photographic and Charting Service

DUFFEL BAG swung over his shoulder, the young airman approached the Orderly Room. His blue uniform was brand-new — so obviously new that you could practically see where the tags had been. He had just arrived at Orlando, Florida, and was reporting to the headquarters of the MATS' Air Photographic and Charting Service.

At the door he set down his duffel, straightened out his uniform, and adjusted his dark blue tie. Confidently he opened the door. Hadn't he just completed basic training? He was now a full-fledged member of the U. S. Air Force.

"Oh, you're one of the new group reporting in for the Geodetic Course," said the Airman 1st class, Charge of Quarters. The newcomer handed him a copy of his orders.

"Follow me," the CQ said, and headed for the closed door on the right. The knock was answered by "Come in," and they both entered.

"Sergeant, this is one of the new men for the 1381st," the Airman 1st said as he passed the copy of the orders to the First Sergeant.

The big man seated behind the desk wore eight blue and white stripes on each sleeve. His youthful appearance belied his thirty-nine years of age.

"I see from your records that you've had plenty of math at college. Well, that's why you were selected for the 1381st Geodetic Squadron."

Looking the new man over carefully, he added, "But first you're going to take a ten-week course with us. Forty per cent of it will be classwork and the rest practical work in the field, and I guarantee that it will make your college days seem like kindergarten. But when you're through, you'll be a qualified 'astrogeodesist.' "

When the First Sergeant had finished with his "lecture," he said, "The CQ will show you your quarters where you'll meet some of the other nineteen members of your class." Then with a smile he concluded, "Welcome to the APCS and good luck!"

As he left the Orderly Room with the CQ, the recruit asked, "What's an 'astrogeodesist'?"

"Well," the CQ hesitated. I'm not a technician. I'm only in the administrative end of this outfit. I don't think you'll find the word in any dictionary, but I've been around here long enough to know that it's a guy whose job is to map the earth, make charts, and measure distances accurately."

"I see," said the newcomer, "and the 'astro' part probably refers to the special applications of the space age."

By this time they had arrived at the barracks and the Airman 3rd was heading back to the Orderly Room. However, before much more time would pass, the new airman would have all the answers.

He and the other members of his class would first learn the conventional method of earth measurement called *triangulation.* Basically, a survey team using a long steel tape accurately lays out a line several miles long. This is called the base line. A telescopic instrument for measuring angles is set up at each end of the base line. The instrument is called a *theodolite* and is the same type of device used by surveyors in laying out roads or determining the boundaries of real estate. In triangulation, both theodolites are aimed at the same object — a third point, several miles away. Since the length of the base line is now known, and the theodolites have measured the angles, the APCS astrogeodesists can compute accurately the length of the other two legs of the triangle by simple geometry. The mapping is continued by shifting one of the theodolites to the new point, whose location has just been determined. This forms a new triangle and the process is repeated. By "leapfrogging" the triangles, in this manner, entire continents can be mapped and measured.

The triangulation system, however, is a long and tedious one. Another drawback of this process is the fact that it is a line of sight system. In other words, there can be no obstacles in the way, such as mountains or jungles. And because triangulation has a range of only several miles, large bodies of water prove to be insurmountable barriers.

But the MATS' Air Photographic and Charting Service has the answer to these problems in the *Hiran* system. This scientific device works over mountainous areas, jungles, larger bodies of water, deserts, polar ice, or what have you. And it can accomplish more in a matter of hours than two dozen ground survey teams, using the triangulation system, can do in weeks.

Here's how it works:

A special, electronically equipped RC-130 Hercules, a reconnaissance version of its cargo-carrying sister, is flown back and forth between a pair of ground stations. The airplane sends signals to the ground receivers which are bounced right back to it. The time lapse between signals is the basis upon which the calculations are made. As in triangulation the system is leapfrogged to cover vast areas.

Simple? Not quite, because APCS men don't just *double-check* — they check and recheck each calculation for a total of twelve times. The Hercules makes six measurements at one altitude and six more at another — and they all must check out.

But Hiran, too, has its limitation. It can only cover a maximum distance of 550 miles between ground stations. This, of course, precludes spanning the oceans. The space age, however, has provided the solution — the geodetic stellar camera.

As in simple triangulation there are two distant stations at precisely known locations, and a third whose measurements are to be determined. A stellar camera is set up at each of the three stations. Then a rocket is fired which releases flares at intervals. The cameras at each of the three stations simultaneously take photos of the rocket's flare. Since two of the locations are known, as well as the precise location of the stars and planets that show up in the photo, the exact location of and distance to the third point can be determined.

But what the space age gave with one hand it took back with the other. This age of rockets and missiles has also given the Air Force astrogeodesists a problem — gravity. For ages, a popular misconception was the belief that the force of gravity was equal at any given spot throughout the globe. There really was no need for anyone to dispute it until the arrival of the space age. Studies have now definitely proved that the force of gravity differs at varied locations. It matters little to the layman, but in the launching of a missile with a thrust of hundreds of thousands of pounds, it could mean the difference between success and failure. Therefore it became the task of the APCS geodesists to measure the force of gravity.

Like all of the MATS operations, the "gravity probe" has also become international in scope. Some fifty-five nations have contributed information to this USAF-sponsored Worldwide Gravity Project.

These, then, are some of the duties that occupy the 1,500 airmen and women of the 1370th Photo Mapping Wing with headquarters at Turner Air Force Base, Georgia. Their jobs carry the six squadrons that make up the Wing to the far corners of the earth. They can be found in remote reaches of the frozen arctic or the steaming tropical jungles of the Amazon – making long-distance measurements, on a regularly scheduled basis, between established geodetic reference systems. They are mapping the world!

Their "little brother," the 1381st Geodetic Survey Squadron at Orlando, has about 250 airmen who work on an "as needed" basis. These skilled technicians furnish precise geodetic survey data on specific projects and assignments as they arise.

Up to this point, we have only heard the story of the "Charting" part of the Air Photographic and Charting Service. Equally as dramatic is the "Photographic" end.

The photo responsibility of the APCS is to record, on film, the many and varied activities of the U.S. Air Force throughout the world.

Their job is to document the daily routine activities of the USAF – the ground crews working on a SAC B-52 bomber; the Air Force Systems Command testing new advanced equipment; gunnery practice with the Tactical Air Command; an Air Defense Command fighter scrambled to intercept a "bogey" – an unidentified aircraft; and a MATS cargo delivery to the USAF terminal at Châteauroux, France.

They are also on duty around the clock, ready and on call to cover special events such as the visit of a VIP, like the President of France to one of our Air Force bases; historical events like the Berlin Airlift; and missile firings. In fact, many of the photos in this book were made by APCS men.

Each and every U.S. missile launching, whether it be from Cape Kennedy in Florida or Vandenberg Air Force Base, California, is photographed by the Air Photographic and Charting Service. Fifteen APCS professional photographers, as well as twenty remotely controlled cameras, record and track every move of the rocket. Within a few hours 4,000 feet of processed and edited color and black-and-white film of the launching are on the way to Air Force engineers and scientists for study and analysis.

APCS is also able to furnish the newspapers with photos of a missile firing within thirty minutes after the rocket left the ground.

In addition to recording events, APCS cameramen are creative, too. They produce all of the Air Force training films, a TV series about the Air Force, monthly newsreels, and feature films. One of these features was acclaimed at three International Film Festivals.

The MATS' Air Photographic and Charting Service photo operations consist of four squadrons. These are based at Orlando; Lookout Mountain, California; St. Louis, Missouri; and Wright-Patterson Air Force Base in Ohio.

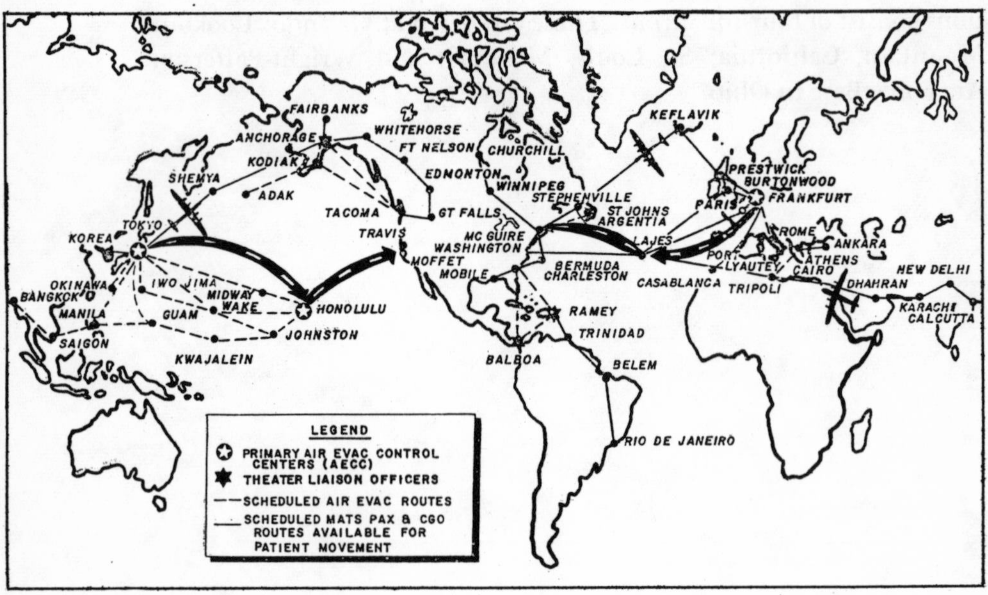
FAIRBANKS
WHITEHORSE
ANCHORAGE
KODIAK
FT NELSON
CHURCHILL
EDMONTON
SHEMYA
ADAK
WINNIPEG
TACOMA
GT FALLS
TOKYO
KOREA
TRAVIS
MOFFET
MC GUIRE
WASHINGTON
MOBILE
OKINAWA
BANGKOK
IWO JIMA
MIDWAY
WAKE
MANILA
GUAM
HONOLULU
SAIGON
JOHNSTON
KWAJALEIN
KEFLAVIK
PRESTWICK
BURTONWOOD
FRANKFURT
STEPHENVILLE
ST JOHNS
ARGENTIA
PARIS
LAJES
ROME
ANKARA
ATHENS
PORT LYAUTEY
CAIRO
NEW DELHI
BERMUDA
CHARLESTON
CASABLANCA
TRIPOLI
DHAHRAN
KARACHI
CALCUTTA
RAMEY
TRINIDAD
BALBOA
BELEM
RIO DE JANEIRO
LEGEND
PRIMARY AIR EVAC CONTROL CENTERS (AECC)
THEATER LIAISON OFFICERS
SCHEDULED AIR EVAC ROUTES
SCHEDULED MATS PAX & CGO ROUTES AVAILABLE FOR PATIENT MOVEMENT

CHAPTER TEN

Wings of Mercy–Aeromedical Evacuation

FLIGHT NURSE'S CREED

I will summon every resource to prevent the triumph of death over life.

I will stand guard over the medicines and equipment entrusted to my care and insure their proper use.

I will be untiring in the performance of my duties and I will remember that, upon my disposition and spirit, will in large measure depend the morale of my patients.

I will be faithful to my training and to the wisdom handed down to me by those who have gone before me.

I have taken a nurse's oath, reverent in man's mind because of the spirit and work of its creator, Florence Nightingale. She, I remember, was called "The Lady with the Lamp."

It is now my privilege to lift this lamp of hope and faith and courage in my profession to heights not known by her in her time. Together with the help of Flight Surgeons and Medical Technicians, I can set the very skies ablaze with life and promise for the sick, injured, and wounded who are my sacred charges.

This I will do. I will not falter in war or in peace.

There was a certain stillness in the air as the aidmen carried the stretchers toward the waiting silver and white aircraft. In its cavernous doorway stood a Flight Nurse, neat and trim in her blue Air Force uniform. On her blouse she wore the silver wings of her profession, and on each shoulder the single silver bar of a first lieutenant.

It was quite unnecessary to caution the medical technicians to exercise care. Well trained, they handled with gentleness their sick and injured charges, who lay helpless on the litters the aidmen were carrying. Still, the Flight Nurse could not help saying: "Easy does it, boys!"

This was the start of a story that is repeated well over three thousand times each year in the continental United States alone. Many more aeromedical evacuation missions take place in our overseas bases all over the world, some finally linking up with the MATS aeromedical evacuation system in the United States.

This is not the story of the Flight Nurse alone, although she is part of it, together with pilot, copilot, engineers, and medical technicians. The "Flight Nurse's Creed," however, holds true for all of them.

Did we say this was the start of the story? Well, not quite. Actually, it had its beginning at any of the numerous locations around the globe where our military or other government personnel are stationed in peacetime — or, in this case, on the battlefield during the Korean War.

The wounded soldiers were given first aid either by their buddies or medics and then moved back to the battalion aid station for further treatment and classification. Those needing additional care were airlifted by helicopter to the Field Hospital. (In some cases they were even taken by helicopter directly from the battlefield.) From the Field Hospital, if their wounds were serious enough, they were evacuated by air to Japan or to the states.

This speedy system of aeromedical evacuation was one of the principal reasons for the reduction of the Korean War death rate among the wounded to 50 per cent that of World War II.

The MATS Aeromedical Evacuation system also airlifted Turkish wounded from Korea to Ankara.

And it succeeded in demonstrating that twenty-one times fewer medical personnel were needed than if the evacuation had been carried out by ship.

During peacetime in overseas areas, accidents and serious illness cases among the military, their dependents, other U.S. government employees, and our Allies are moved by air in theater evacuation aircraft. They are taken to the Casualty Staging Units at the principal aerial ports of embarkation, such as Rhein/Main Airport in Germany. From here the regular MATS cargo planes which have just brought in supplies or passengers from the U.S.A. are converted for Aeromedical Evacuation for the return trip – home.

Today the giant four-jet engine C-135 – the military version of the commercial airliner Boeing 707 – makes this "airevac" run from Rhein/Main in Frankfurt, Germany, to McGuire Air Force Base near Trenton, New Jersey, in only eight hours. This journey used to take as long as twenty-four hours – a full day – in the C-121 Super Connies and in the Douglas DC 6B (known by the USAF as the C-118 Liftmaster).

Once back in the continental United States they are in the capable hands of the MATS 1405th Aeromedical Transport Wing, formerly the 1st Aeromedical Transport Group. MATS, which itself has an enviable safety record, had to take a backseat to the 1st AMTG because it claimed to have "the carefulest pilots in MATS" – with *no accidents at all.*

The Wing flies the Convair C-131 Samaritan, an aircraft specifically designed for the tough and exacting job of aeromedical evacuation. It is also the Air Force's first fully pressurized twin-engine transport. To all intents and purposes, it is a "flying hospital ward," completely all-weather air-conditioned and equipped with oxygen for the patients. It is also geared to carry such bulky medical equipment as iron lungs and chest respirators.

In addition to the regular flying crew of three, the Samaritan has a medical staff consisting of the Flight Nurse and two Medical Technicians. It is their job to care for as many as 40 ambulatory patients, or 27 litter patients, or combinations of both, in this 10-by-40-foot "airborne ward." Needless to say, this is a bigger operation and a greater responsibility than the customary land-based hospital ward because "airevac" patients can run the gamut from accident cases requiring plasma to a little boy with polio, in an iron lung, or to patients with dozens of other maladies including communicable diseases, injuries, psychoses, and other complications – and all in the same ward.

The Samaritan operates at altitudes of over 20,000 feet, travels at more than 230 mph, and has a range of over 1,000 miles. It has a large 6-by-8-foot litter loading hatch to accommodate the stretcher cases. Ambulatory patients and the crew use a built-in folding passenger stairway on the opposite side.

The Aeromedical Transport Wing boasts that, "no sick or wounded man is more than twenty-four hours away from the best medical care in the world."

And they live up to it!

Here is how they do it:

The Wing operates what they call "trunk lines" across the United States. These main line or express routes connect the two ports of aerial debarkation — McGuire Air Force Base in New Jersey and Travis Air Force Base in California, with Scott Air Force Base in Illinois and Kelly Air Force Base in Texas. Operating from each of these express stops are "feeder routes" which cover all of the local stops in between, and link up the entire continental network.

Day in and day out, each day of the year (there are no holidays in aeromedical evacuation), every few minutes around the clock, one of the 1405th's gleaming silver and white Samaritans with a big bright red cross on its rudder, either lands or takes off with a patient load. This aerial-medical shuttle system picks up patients as well as delivers them. They service more than 600 Army, Navy, Air Force, Veterans Administration, Public Health Service, and other government hospitals, using over 400 military and commercial airfields.

Once a patient arrives in the continental U.S.A., there are two considerations determining where he will be sent. The primary concern is his diagnosis — where can he best be treated for the particular ailment he has? The next consideration is locating him in a hospital nearest to his home.

Let's see what would happen to those patients that have just arrived at McGuire from Germany in the C-135 jet. Those whose destinations were in the northeast would be shifted to one of the Samaritans operating on that local feeder route. For example, a patient going to the Walter Reed General Hospital in Washington, D.C., would be "off-loaded" at Andrews Air Force Base. Here he would be met by an ambulance or, in emergency cases, by a helicopter.

The rest of the patients would be placed aboard one of the Samaritans operating on the trunk line. Patients for midwestern stops would be debarked at Scott, and transferred to the proper "feeder" plane. Others would be evacuated to Kelly for southern destinations, while still others would be delivered to Travis for far western stops.

The entire continental "airevac" operation was masterminded from the 1st AMTG Headquarters at Brooks Air Force Base, near San Antonio, Texas, from 1948 to 1964. Now the 1405th Aeromedical Transport Wing, it keeps tabs on the five Aeromedical Evacuation squadrons and their 17 C-131 Samaritans. From their new headquarters at Scott Air Force Base, Illinois, these operate from southern California to the northern tip of Maine, and numerous points in between, to cover the entire country. They know where each plane is at all times, and they know the location and destination of each one of over 40,000 patients a year while they are in their care. For an emergency pickup they can divert an aircraft, and are completely flexible in their operations — always keeping in mind that "24-hour" deadline.

In addition to their regular military duties, the 1405th carries civilians in emergencies. They have an arrangement with the National Foundation to fly polio patients on a "cost" reimbursable basis. They even fly special teams overseas to bring back polio patients.

In military parlance, every patient is a VIP and gets the "red carpet" treatment. In short, everything is done "to prevent the triumph of death over life."

Aeromedical evacuation actually had its embryonic beginning in February, 1918, during World War I, when a converted Curtis JN-4 Jenny carried the first litter patient in aviation history. But that was a far cry from today's custom-built C-131 Samaritan with its completely equipped and staffed "flying hospital ward," or the sleek C-135 Stratolifter jet.

CHAPTER ELEVEN

MATS and Missiles

"SEE THEM loading that Atlas missile into the Cargomaster?" asked the captain.

The young lieutenant looked in the direction the captain had pointed and nodded in agreement. "Yes, sir, but who is that fellow who seems to be in charge of the show over there?"

"Oh him! That's the 'Birdwatcher.' You know, a missile is called a 'bird' and he's the man who's responsible for it while it's in transit. So put *bird* and *watcher* together and you've got the 'Birdwatcher.' It's as simple as that."

The Birdwatcher, strategically positioned to the rear of the giant transport, signals to the crew operating the lift aboard the aircraft and the massive Atlas missile begins to move steadily up the tracks into the rear of the 143-ton MATS Cargomaster. All 75 feet of the ICBM, under the careful scrutiny of the Birdwatcher, is drawn steadily through the rear mounted doors of the big aircraft. These doors open in four directions and like everything else about the C-133 were designed to accommodate such outsize cargo.

However, once the missile is aboard, the Birdwatcher's job does not cease. He is still responsible for monitoring the missile's delicate instruments while in flight and to supervise the unloading of the "bird."

Hauling missiles by air is the practical way to do the job, particularly when compared to land transportation. Trucking a big missile such as Atlas from the manufacturer in San Diego, California, to Cape Kennedy, Florida, is a tremendous job. By air the trip lasts only a few short hours, but the journey by truck takes at least two weeks. Moreover, a large crew of specialists and technicians is required on an overland haul because the risks are so much greater than by air.

First the route must be carefully planned and checked to avoid narrow roads, bridges that cannot hold the excess weight of the missile and transporter, tunnels that are too low for clearance, and other obstacles. Once under way the giant missile-carrying trailer must be escorted in the front and rear by vehicles loaded with Air Police to safeguard the security of the weapon and to direct traffic blocked by the slow-moving caravan.

Were it not for MATS, this overland method of transporting missiles would be the only other practical way. As a matter of fact, MATS has the only two types of aircraft in the world large enough and properly equipped and constructed to handle large military missiles such as Atlas, Titan, and Minuteman. These are the C-133 and the smaller C-124 Globemaster which, unlike the former, loads straight in from the front through great clamshell doors.

Not only are these aircraft specifically geared for physically handling and carrying missiles, the temperature and atmospheric conditions are also controlled to protect their sensitive instruments. And the pilots and navigators plan their missions as close to flight time as possible to take advantage of the best weather. They go miles out of their way to avoid turbulence which might cause stress.

Carrying an Atlas missile from the west coast to the east coast of the United States is a journey of some 2,500 miles although strictly within continental limits. In November, 1958, MATS airlifted Thor IRBM's and their equipment from Santa Monica, California, across the U.S.A. and the Atlantic Ocean to England, flying a record of 80 missions. The following year MATS also airlifted a 52-ton Atlas ICBM and 100 tons of other equipment over the Atlantic to the USAF display at the International Air Show in Paris.

In addition to the "big ones," MATS also carries the smaller missiles, such as the Polaris, Bomarc, Pershing, Sergeant, Redstone — in fact, every missile in the entire U.S. arsenal.

MATS is closely tied in with the United States space program and has been from the start. Charged with the logistical support of the Atlantic Missile Range, MATS aircraft cover the 9,000-mile "shooting gallery" which extends through the Caribbean, the South Atlantic, to the Indian Ocean. MATS carries personnel, mail, and equipment between Cape Kennedy, Florida, and Pretoria, South Africa. Stops on the way include the islands of Grand Bahama, Eleuthera, San Salvador, Mayaguana, Grand Turk, Antigua, St. Lucia, Fernando de Noronha, and Ascension.

Polaris submarines are also serviced by MATS. These nuclear-powered subs have the ability to remain submerged for a much longer period of time than the conventionally powered diesel engine type. Because of this fact and the added strain placed upon its personnel, each Polaris sub has two complete crews to staff it. These Blue and Gold crews alternate, and MATS airlifts the crew that's on duty to its overseas base and returns the off-duty crew to the United States.

In supporting the entire United States missile program, MATS carries a great volume of cargo. For example, in one year alone – 1963 – MATS airlifted 32,000 tons of Navy and Air Force missile cargo. This was accomplished in some 839 airlift missions from the manufacturers' facilities to test sites or to operational launching pads.

CHAPTER TWELVE

MATS Aircraft

THE STORY OF MATS is the story of men and machines. This chapter deals with the machines — those mighty and versatile aircraft with which the Military Air Transport Service performs its many and varied tasks.

In its principal function — the global airlift mission — MATS has used many types of aircraft ranging from the old faithful World War II twin-engine C-47 "Gooney Bird" and the C-46 Curtis Commando to the four-jet C-135, military version of the Boeing 707. Also in the works for delivery by 1965 is the other long-awaited "C-jet," the Lockheed C-141. This giant four-jet strategic cargo carrier is being custom built for MATS. It has approximately twice the capacity of its current predecessor, the C-130 Hercules, a giant in its own right. Air Evac has the C-131A Samaritan, the tailor-made "flying hospital ward" specifically designed for the transporting of sick and wounded.

Each of the MATS Technical Services has its own specialized aircraft. Air Rescue has its versatile helicopters and the HU-16 Albatross amphibians; the Air Weather Service is equipped with rugged converted bombers for flying into hurricanes; and the Air Photo and Charting Service has its specialized photo reconnaissance aircraft. Like AWS, the APCS and ARS also used converted bombers for their missions.

Just as all types of Air Force aircraft carry a type letter identifying their primary function and particular mission, such as *F* for Fighter (F-86 Sabrejet), and *B* for Bomber (B-58 Hustler), so, too, do the MATS aircraft.

All of the MATS airlift aircraft carry the letter designation *C*, which indicates transport or cargo and includes both passenger and freight carriers with a pay-load capacity greater than 2,000 pounds.

Therefore the Globemaster is the C-124 and the C-130E is the Hercules.

Often the MATS function is indicated by a prefix letter before the regular Air Force type letter. The *V* such as in the VC-137 designates a staff transport plane for VIP's, such as visiting foreign dignitaries. One example might be the President's aircraft. These are generally part of the Special Air Missions (SAM) unit.

Until 1963, Air Rescue Service aircraft carried an *S* for "Search and Rescue" in front of their regular Air Force letter. Therefore an SH-19 was a Rescue Helicopter and an SA-16 Albatross was a Rescue Amphibian. Cargo aircraft converted for rescue purposes included the SC-47 and SC-54. Changes have been made, however, and the prefix letter *H* for "Help" has taken the place of the *S*. Another change has traded the *A* formerly designating "amphibian" to *U* for "utility." So now the SA-16 is known as the HU-16.

A *W* added to the designation stands for "Weather" and indicates an Air Weather Service aircraft having permanently installed meteorological equipment. An example of this was the WB-29, a weather version of the B-29 Superfortress bomber. By the same token, the addition of an *R* to the original letter identification, as in the RB-50, singles out a "Reconnaissance" or photo plane of the Air Photo and Charting Service. In this case it is the four-engine Superfortress bomber, modified by the permanent installation of photo or electronic reconnaissance equipment.

Considered an integral part of the MATS strategic airlift capability, rather than one of the Technical Services, Air Evacuation aircraft carry no additional letter other than the standard *C* as in the C-131 Samaritan.

Described in these pages and a photo section are most of the principal types of MATS aircraft — past, present, and future — along with background history and some pertinent specifications and data. Mileage and airspeed figures are expressed in statute miles. These are the same miles consisting of 5,280 feet used in everyday conversation.

Some of the photos of early MATS aircraft show them with the words *Atlantic, Pacific,* or *Continental* across their vertical stabilizers and rudders. These serve as a historical record since they were taken before the changeover to *EASTAF* and *WESTAF*. There is no present counterpart for the *Continental* Division which formerly followed scheduled routes across the United States.

General Descriptions of MATS Global Airlift Aircraft

C-141 Starlifter

Wide-sweeping wings indicate this giant's mission – airlifting huge military loads across long reaches of the world's oceans and continents. The C-141 Starlifter, approximately twice the capacity of the Hercules, was rolled out for display on August 22, 1963. Its first flight was completed successfully in December, 1963, and it will join the Military Air Transport Service global airlift force in the spring of 1965. Capable of airlifting 50,000 pounds 4,600 miles nonstop, or 20,000 pounds between California and Japan (6,325 miles), its versatility includes airlifting 154 fully equipped combat troops or 80 patients. An all-jet 500-mph aircraft, with wide rear doors for big cargo, it dwarfs the tiny Wright Flyer, the first military air transport built in 1908.

C-130 Hercules

The extended-range Lockheed C-130E Hercules provides valuable interim modernization to the airlift force of MATS. The first several were delivered in August, 1962, and MATS now has more than 100.

Refinements over the C-130B, already in service, give the high-winged Hercules 10 tons more gross takeoff weight — 155,000 pounds. Also, additional fuel tanks (between the nacelles of the turboprop engines), which each carry 1,360 gallons, enable the "E" version to fly the Atlantic nonstop with normal loads, and the Pacific with one stop. Rear loading at truck-bed height, ability to land and take off from comparatively short runways, and a relatively high speed (more than 300 mph) all make this aircraft valuable for global airlift tasks, including training for assault airdrop of combat paratroops.

These C-130E aircraft will help fill MATS' needs even after pure-jet aircraft designed specifically for cargo are available in mid-1965. Its normal load is about 16 tons and it can carry 92 combat troops or 74 litter patients or 64 paratroops.

C-135 Stratolifter

The Boeing C-135 Stratolifter is the first pure-jet cargo aircraft in military service. The 500-mph aircraft, with nonstop over-ocean range, can fly at twice the speed, twice the height, and can carry three times the load for a 50 per cent greater range than most airplanes MATS currently uses. It can carry 38,000 pounds of pay load 3,600 miles at 40,000 feet. Basic crew is six.

The aircraft, similar to the Boeing 707, is slightly smaller in most dimensions. Primarily a cargo carrier, it can be converted to carry troops or litter patients. It is the only aircraft now used for aeromedical evacuation from overseas points to the United States. The first aircraft was delivered to MATS in June, 1961. More than half of the C-135's in service with MATS have turbofan engines for greater range and lift.

C-133 Cargomaster

The Douglas C-133 Cargomaster, originally named Globemaster III, is the largest aircraft in the MATS global airlift inventory. Designed to handle outsized cargo, the Cargomaster can airlift all U.S. operational missiles. With it, MATS has cut delivery time from manufacturer to launch site to hours instead of days required by overland hauling.

In December, 1958, a C-133 established the world's record for a single cargo airlift. It flew 118,000 pounds of cargo to an altitude of 10,000 feet, topping previous records by 40,000 pounds. The plane continually demonstrates its tremendous capacity by carrying everything from giant missiles to rocket launchers.

The Cargomaster normally operates between 15,000 and 30,000 feet, cruising at nearly 300 mph. With a 20-ton pay load, its range is more than 3,700 miles. It carries a basic crew of five and is powered by four Pratt and Whitney T-34 turboprop engines developing 6,000 equivalent shaft horsepower each. These aircraft are assigned to Dover Air Force Base, Delaware, and to Travis Air Force Base, California.

C-124 Globemaster II

The Douglas C-124 Globemaster is the backbone of MATS' airlift force. Introduced to MATS in June, 1950, it has been in on every major airlift since Korea. It has even become a missile carrier, airlifting the Thor IRBM and its component parts to England for RAF use.

This aircraft flew cargo airdrop missions for seven consecutive years in Operation Deep Freeze, the resupply of scientific stations in the Antarctic. It bore the brunt of the Chile, Congo, and Cuba air-

C-141 STARLIFTER

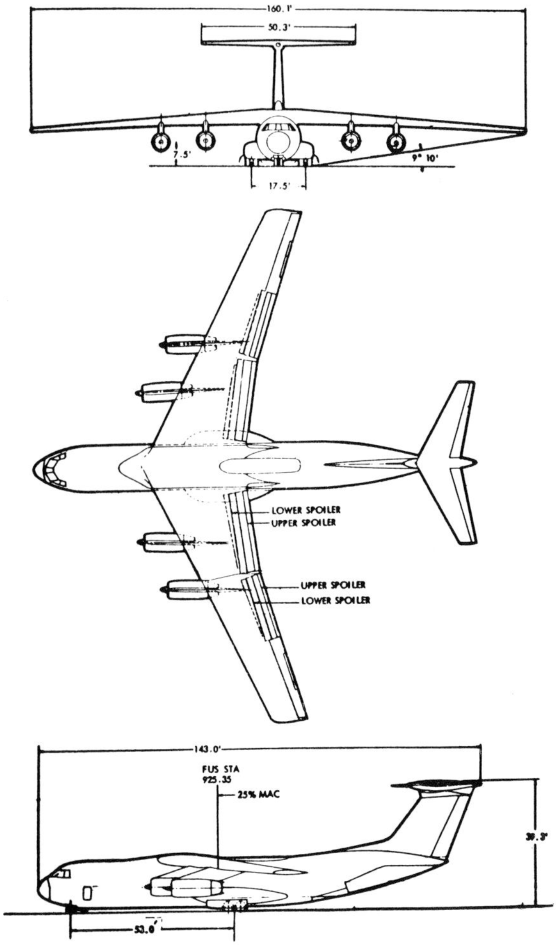

C-103E HERCULES

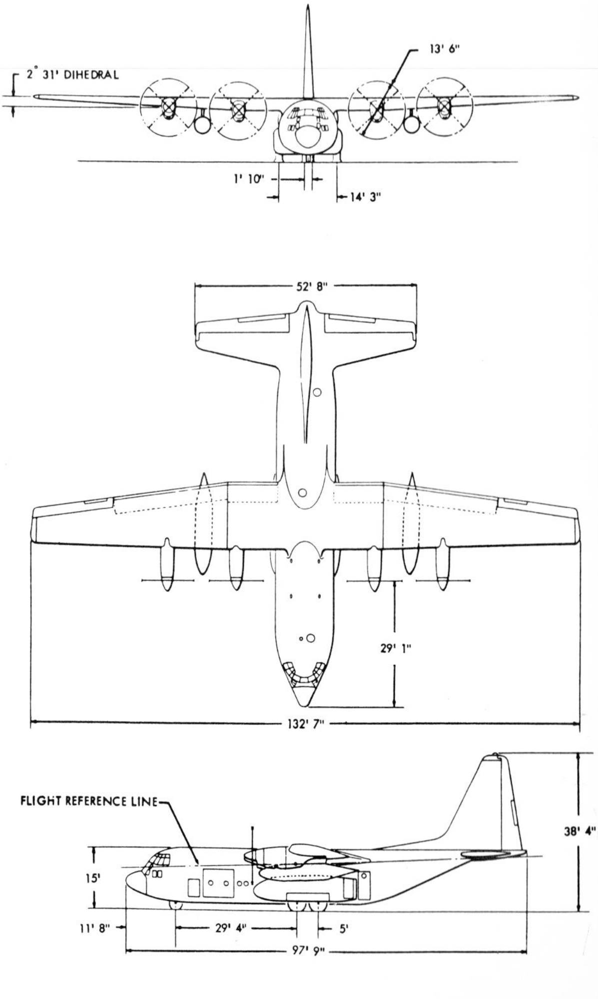

C-135 STRATOLIFTER

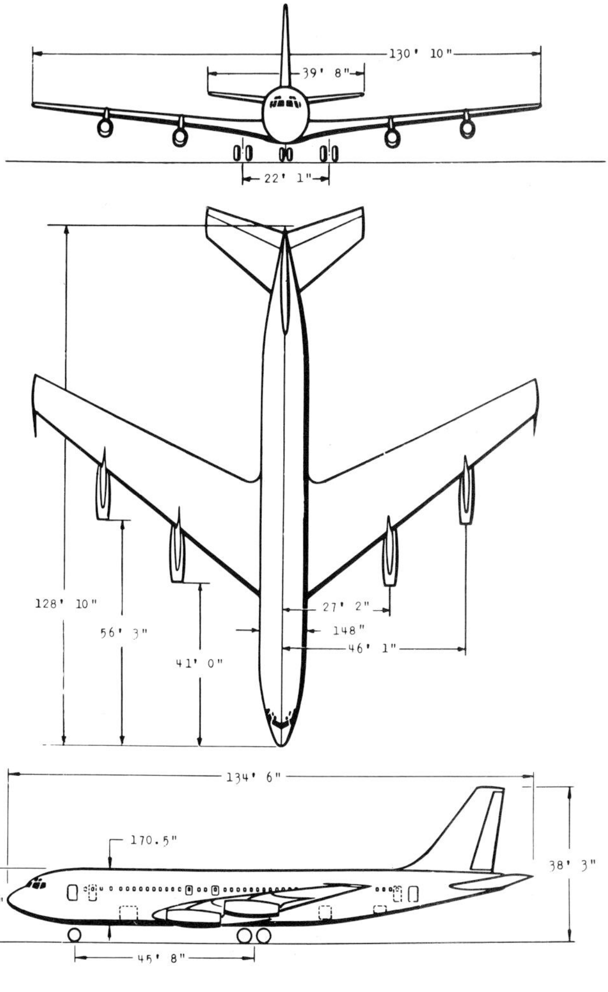

C-133 CARGOMASTER

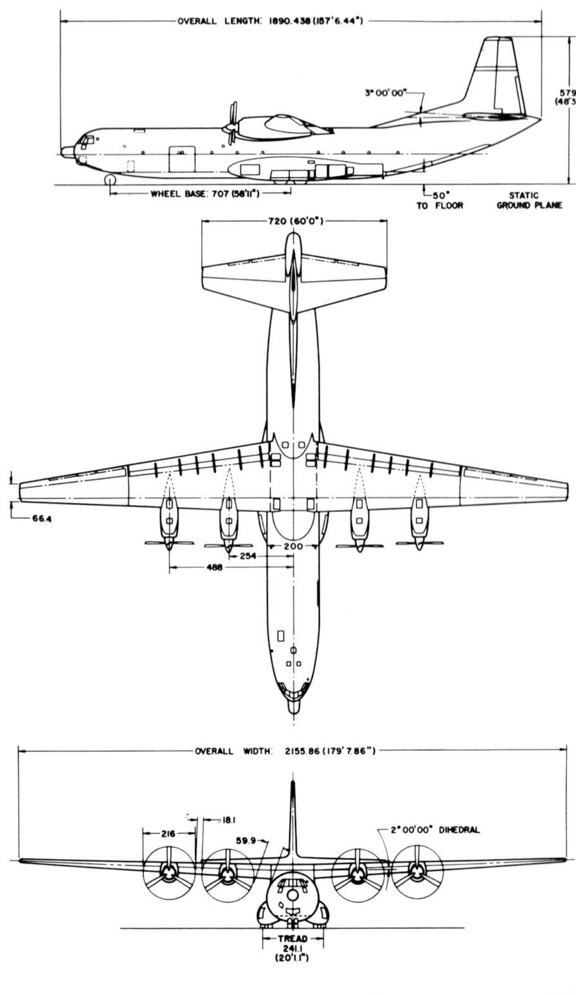

C-124 GLOBEMASTER

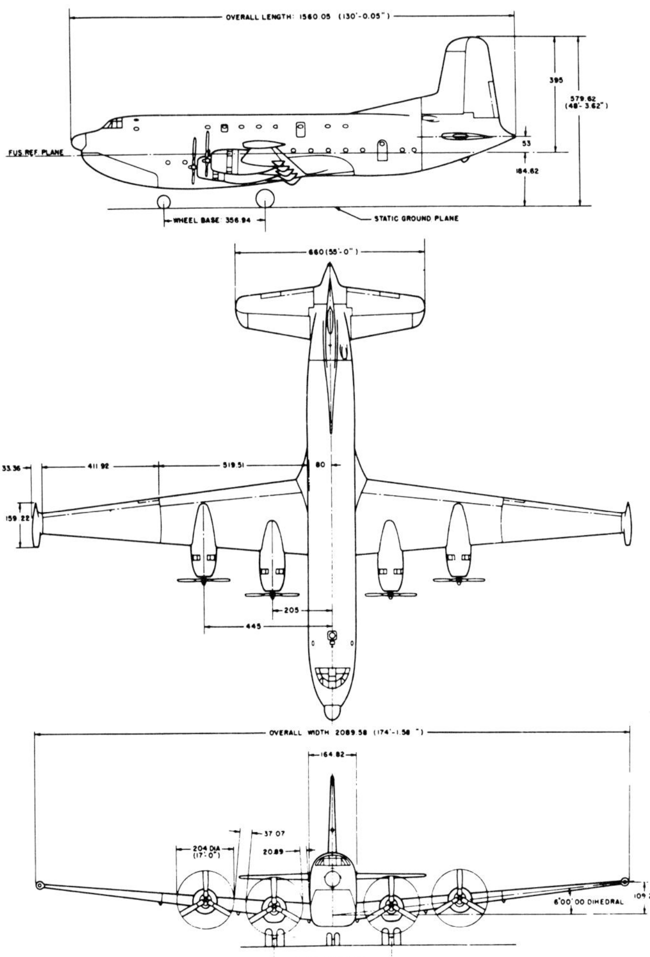

C-118 LIFTMASTER

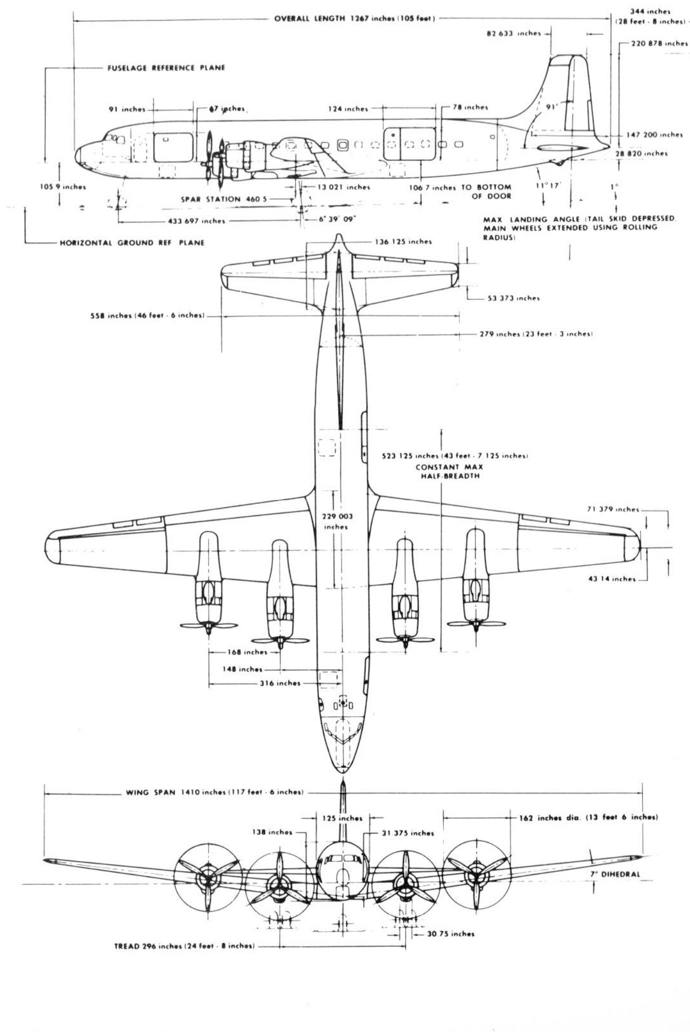

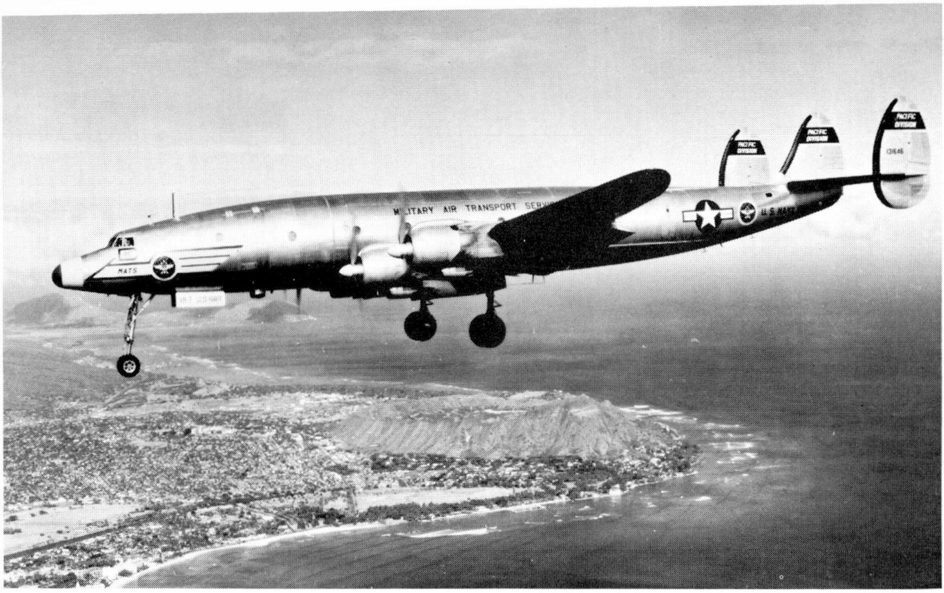

C-121 SUPER CONSTELLATION

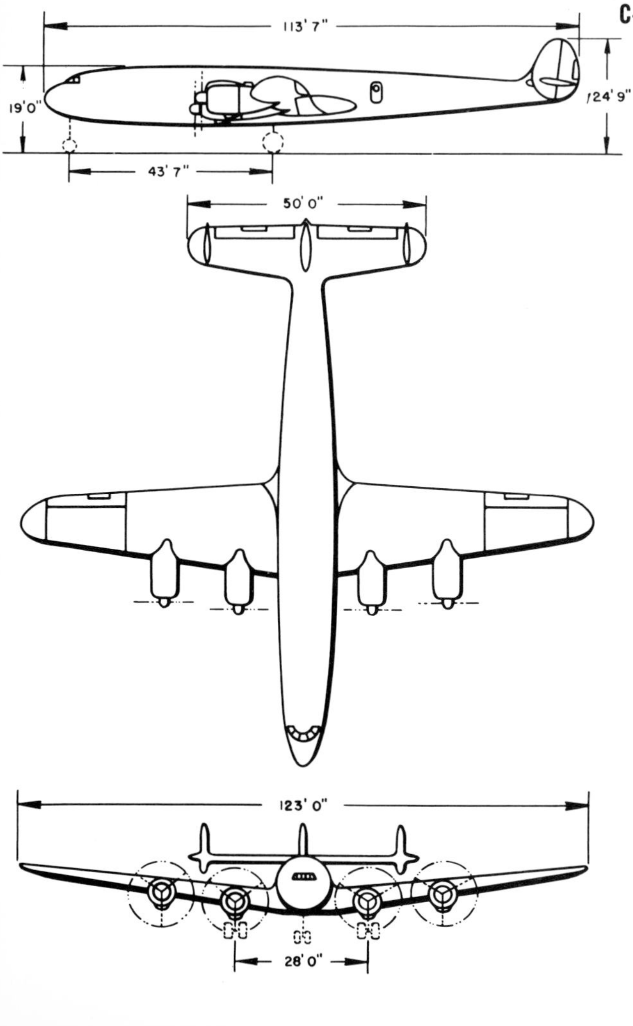

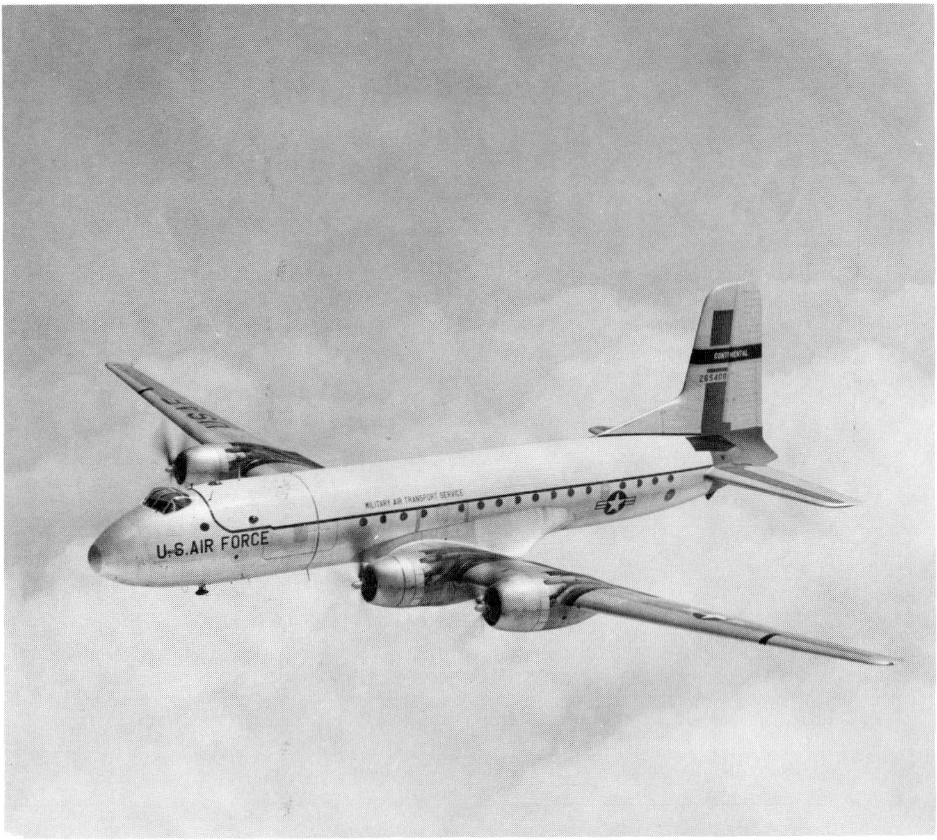

C-74 GLOBEMASTER I

C-97 STRATOFREIGHTER

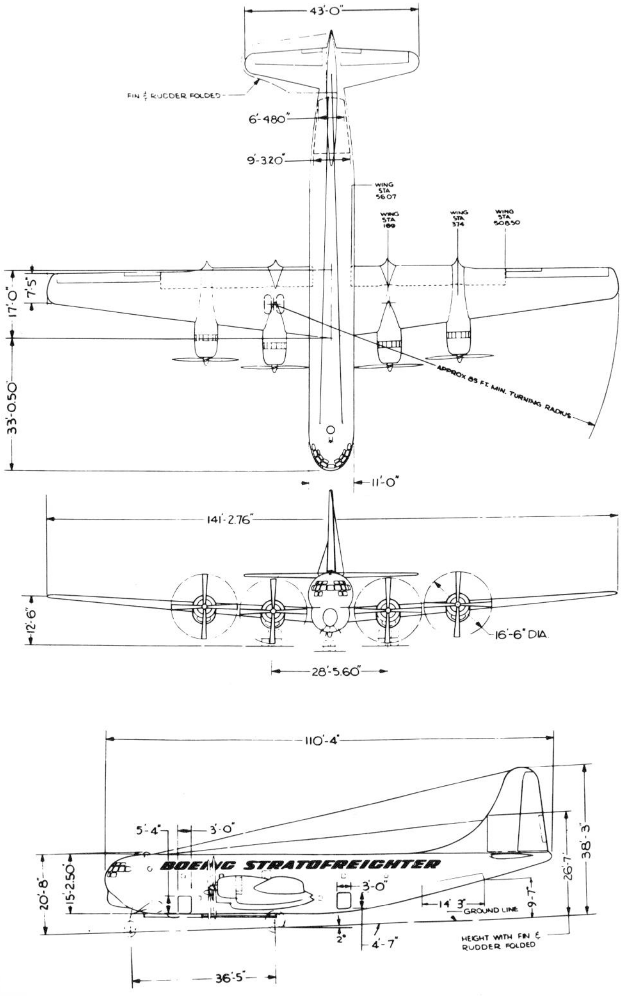

C-54 SKYMASTER

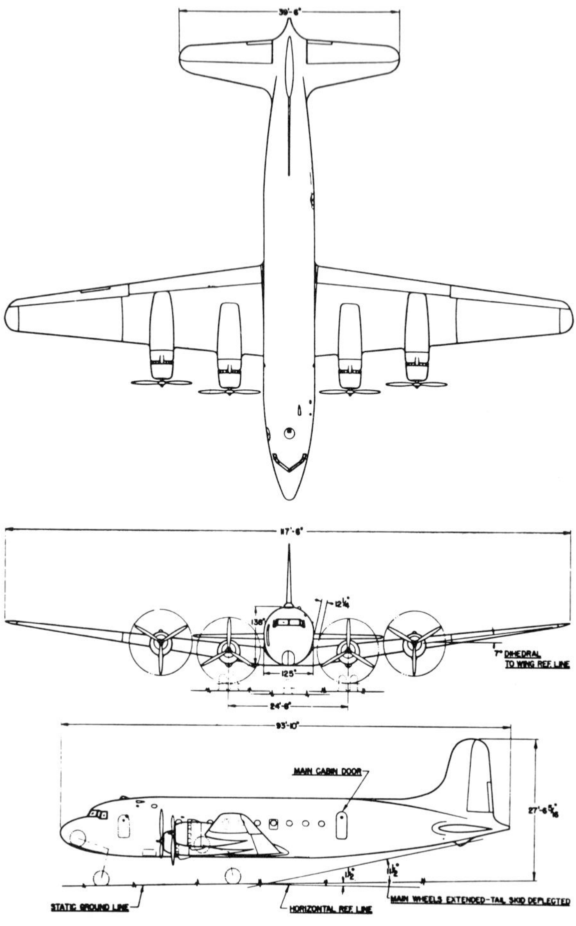

C-47 SKYTRAIN

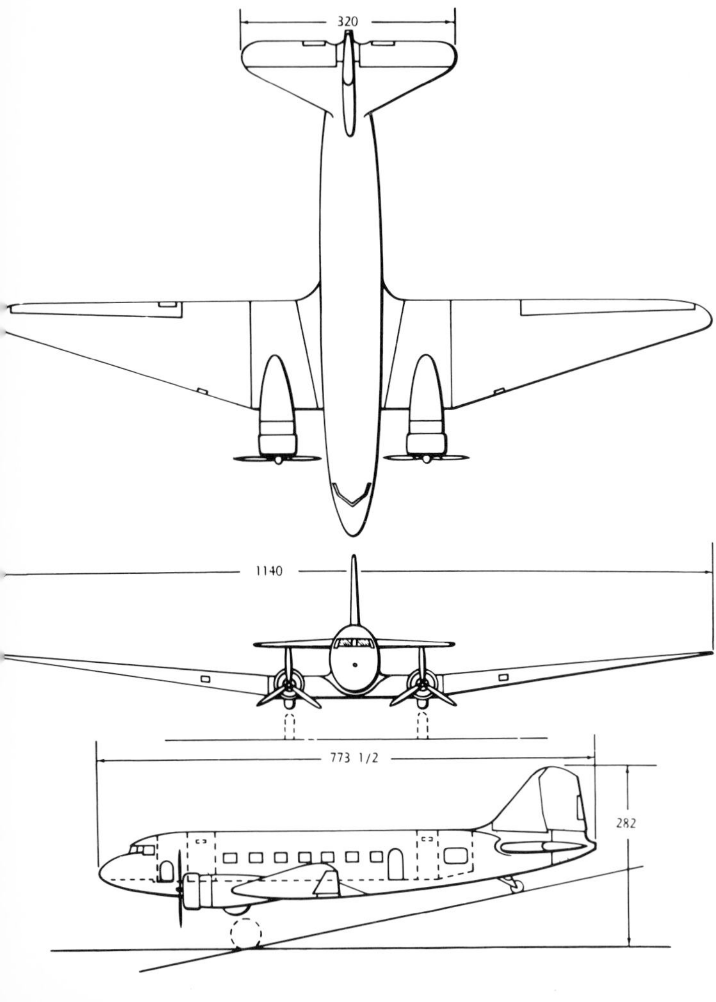

C-131 SAMARITAN

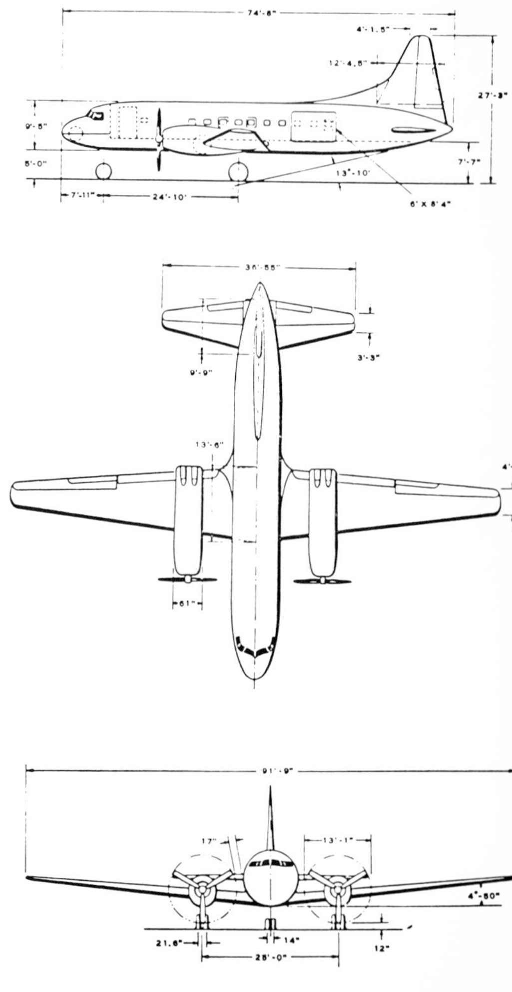

VC-137

VC-140 JETSTAR

RC-130 HERCULES

HH-43 HUSKIE

HH-19 CHICKASAW

SH-21 WORKHORSE

HU-16 ALBATROSS

SB-17 FLYING FORTRESSES (right and left)

SB-29 SUPERFORTRESS (center)

WB-47 STRATOJET

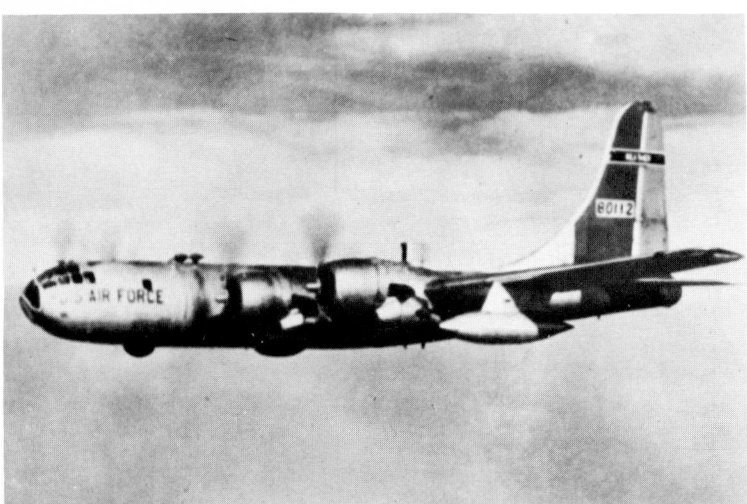

WB-50 SUPERFORTRESS

lifts, and is now being used by MATS in training for assault airdrop of combat paratroops.

It can carry 200 fully equipped combat troops or 127 litter patients or a 20-ton cargo pay load. With this load, it has a range of 1,808 miles. Its speed is 230 mph at a normal cruise altitude of 7,000 to 10,000 feet. Its four Pratt and Whitney piston engines develop 3,800 horsepower each. The basic crew is six.

C-118 Liftmaster

The Douglas C-118 Liftmaster, one of the very dependable combat troop and cargo aircraft in MATS, joined the airlift force in September, 1952. It made the first MATS nonstop flight across the Atlantic in early 1954. The Liftmaster had a key role in Operation Safe Haven when 14,000 Hungarian refugees were airlifted to the U.S. in late 1956 and early 1957. The large four-engine transport is a direct lineal descendant of the C-47 and C-54. On commercial airlines it is known as the DC-6B.

The aircraft can carry 60 combat troops and their equipment and can deliver them within a range of 2,760 miles. It cruises at 18,000 feet at 276 mph. Basic crew is seven.

C-121 Super Constellation

The Lockheed C-121 Super Constellation joined MATS in 1953 and has been used as a convertible carrier for both cargo and personnel. It flew both oceans from its two bases of operation, Charleston Air Force Base, South Carolina, and Moffett Naval Air Station, California. Besides normal troop and cargo operations, the C-121 was used on the State Department "embassy runs" operating into South America. A C-121 served as President Eisenhower's personal aircraft, the *Columbine*. Super Connies flown by the MATS Navy Squadron were designated R7V's.

The C-121 cruises at 17,000 feet at 282 mph and carries a basic crew of eight. All the Super Constellations could be converted for troop, cargo, or air evacuation missions. It can carry 76 fully equipped troops over a 3,050-mile range. These are being phased out of the force in favor of the C-130E. The C-121 is easily recognized from its triple bank of fins and rudders.

C-74 Globemaster I

Forerunner of today's Globemaster C-124 was the Douglas C-74.

The four-engine transport carried large pay loads of cargo and personnel on the MATS global routes in the late 1940's and early 1950's. This particular C-74 was assigned to what was then known as the Continental Division which had routes across the United States. Scheduled flights over continental United States, however, are no longer made by MATS. Also named the Globemaster, it was the military version of the DC-7.

C-97 Stratofreighter

Boeing's twin-deck, heavy-duty C-97 Stratofreighter (also called Stratocruiser) was designed as a pressurized, long-range air transport of bulky cargoes at high speeds. The dependable MATS transport had a built-in loading ramp to facilitate handling of howitzers, ambulances, and other mobile equipment. Normal cruising speed on MATS flights was 270 mph with a cargo capacity of 68,500 pounds, or 130 fully equipped troops. C-97's were also used extensively as patient air evacuation planes in the Pacific area and could carry 79 litter patients, attendants, and supplies. Maximum speed was 350 mph.

C-54 Skymaster

Big sister of the C-47 was the Douglas C-54 known on the commercial airlines as the DC-4. This four-engine Skymaster was used on the Air Transport Command's Atlantic crossings during World War II. With a range of more than 3,000 miles they were also used on U.S. continental routes for "express" runs. Like the C-47 it joined MATS when the ATC and NATS teamed up to become MATS in 1948. The Skymaster bore the brunt of the Berlin Airlift.

C-47 Skytrain

"Old Faithful" of air transports was the C-47 Douglas Skytrain, designated the Dakota by the RAF and more popularly called the "Gooney Bird." From 1932, for a period of over twenty years, this twin-engine workhorse was a mainstay of the civilian airlines. As the DC-3 it was one of the best-known and most widely used American commercial aircraft. It is also a World War II veteran of the Hump operation, where with the Air Transport Command, the MATS predecessor, it carried supplies from India over the high Himalayan Mountains into China.

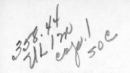

General Descriptions of MATS Specialized Aircraft

Aeromedical Evacuation

C-131 Samaritan

The Convair C-131 is used by MATS primarily as a flying "hospital ward" between military hospitals in the United States. The first twin-engine, fully pressurized transport in the USAF inventory, it is used by aeromedical evacuation units of MATS and can carry 40 ambulatory or 27 litter patients. It has a speed of 230 mph, a range of more than 1,000 miles, and can operate above 20,000 feet. Fifteen similar aircraft were also used by Special Air Missions to carry VIP's on short to medium range trips.

Special Air Missions (SAM)

VC-137

Assigned to the Special Air Missions 1254th Air Transport Wing, Washington, D.C., this military version of the Boeing 707 is used to move top government and military officials. It can fly above 40,000 feet at more than 600 mph. It is a sister ship of the C-135 Stratolifter.

VC-140 Jetstar

The small Lockheed VC-140 Jetstar has two engines clustered on each side of the fuselage near the tail. MATS has ten in the 1254th Air Transport Wing, Washington, D.C., to move top government and military officials. It carries eight passengers, two crew members, has a range of about 1,900 miles, 500-mph speed, and flies to altitudes up to 45,000 feet. It was the first U.S. jet utility aircraft and replaced Special Air Missions' piston engine C-131.

Air Photographic and Charting Service

RC-130 Hercules

This Lockheed aircraft, equipped with the latest electronic aerial survey equipment, is used by the 1370th Photo Mapping Group of MATS' Air Photographic and Charting Service. The turboprop plane has a ceiling of more than 30,000 feet, a 2,000-mile range, and flies over 350 mph. Except for the specialized reconnaissance equipment within, it closely resembles the global airlift C-130.

Air Rescue Service (ARS)

HH-43B Husky

These twin-rotor, turbine-powered helicopters are assigned to the MATS Air Rescue Service. This Kaman helicopter has a useful load of 1,200 pounds, a range of 190 miles, and a speed of about 125 mph. It can hover in midair or land in otherwise inaccessible places. It can carry six ambulatory patients or four litter patients.

HH-19 Chickasaw

One of the most utilitarian aircraft in the Air Rescue Service, this Sikorsky helicopter had a useful load of 1,800 pounds, a range of 500 miles, and a speed of 112 mph. It could hover motionless or land in otherwise inaccessible places. It was able to carry eight ambulatory patients or six litter cases. To aid pickups, it had a hydraulic-electric hoist and 100-foot cable and sling to haul up survivors. HH-19 crews were the first to administer in-flight plasma transfusions, and to fly helicopters from the U.S. across the North Atlantic to Europe in 1952.

HH-21 Workhorse

Another of the ARS rotary wing rescue aircraft is the HH-21 capable of carrying 20 troops or 12 litter patients plus attendants. This Vertol helicopter is larger than the Sikorsky SH-19 and has rotor blades mounted in tandem – one set in the front and another in the rear. It was dubbed the "Flying Banana" by the troops.

HU-16 Albatross

The Grumman amphibian is the backbone of MATS' Air Rescue Service. Capable of landing on choppy water and of short, jet assisted takeoffs, the Albatross is used by ARS throughout the world. In use since 1947, it has a 2,500-mile range, a 212-mph speed, and can carry ten passengers.

SB-17 Flying Fortress and SB-29 Superfortress

The tables are turned! In the Air Rescue Service giant bombers become "angels of mercy." The photo shows two SB-17's, on either flank, escorting an SB-29. Each of the former World War II bomber types carried large lifeboats suspended below the fuselage. They were dropped by parachute to shipwreck or crash survivors at sea.

Air Weather Service

WB-47 Stratojet

Here another bomber does duty as a Weather plane. This WB-47 is a modification of the Strategic Air Command's Stratojet bomber. The six-jet aircraft cruises at better than 600 mph and is used by the Air Weather Service for studying the problems of "all-weather" jet operations at high altitudes as well as in climatological research. They are flown over the Pacific and Atlantic oceans on regularly scheduled weather reconnaissance and hurricane hunting missions.

WB-50 Superfortress

The Boeing WB-50 is used for weather reconnaissance and hurricane hunting by MATS Air Weather Service. It has special electronic weather gear and often flies into the middle of storms for data. It has a range of up to 6,000 miles, a cruising speed of 210 mph, and a ceiling of 40,000 feet.

Appendixes

APPENDIX A

Highlights and Sidelights on Aircraft of the Military Air Transport Service

- A Military Air Transport Service C-133 Cargomaster could carry ten standard-size American automobiles at one time, and still have room to squeeze in another ten "economy" cars.

- Military Air Transport Service's C-133 Cargomaster carries enough fuel to run the average passenger car around the world ten times.

- The entire population (6,000) of Scott Air Force Base, Illinois, home for headquarters of the Military Air Transport Service (MATS), could be airlifted by 30 MATS C-124 Globemasters at the same time.

- Two Military Air Transport Service C-133 Cargomasters can haul as much cargo in the same interval of time as a World War II liberty ship.

- The tail section of a Military Air Transport Service C-133 Cargomaster stands as high as a five-story building.

- A fully loaded Military Air Transport Service C-133 Cargomaster can span the Atlantic from New York to Paris in 12 hours, a distance which would take 62 hours for an automobile averaging 50 mph, and 147 hours for a troopship averaging 18 knots (20.7 mph).

- A Military Air Transport Service C-133 Cargomaster can airlift enough troops to fill three and one-third standard railway passenger cars.

- One Military Air Transport Service C-124 Globemaster could carry 45 average-size American families and their luggage.

- During the peak month of the Berlin Airlift (July, 1949), the airlift task force delivered 253,090 tons of supplies to Berlin using 27,478 flights. The C-141, carrying its MATS-imposed pay-load capacity of 35 tons, could have handled the same tonnage with 7,231 flights (little more than one-quarter as many). Also, the Starlifter could have made the flights two and one-half times faster and been on the ground less time because of its advanced straight-in loading feature.

APPENDIX B

A Capsule History of 30 Days in the Life of a MATS Jet Transport

THIS IS the story of the first 30 days in the global airlift life of a Military Air Transport Service C-135 Stratolifter jet.

The story began in 1961 when John F. Kennedy became President of the United States, for one of his first steps was to begin modernizing America's military airlift.

Within a month of his taking office, contracts were assigned to aircraft manufacturers. One went to Boeing. It called for swift, 600-mph Stratolifter jets.

Four months later the first of the Stratolifters was delivered to the Air Force. It was a military version of the Boeing 707 jetliner which had been tested in over a million flights.

Lt. Gen. Joe W. Kelly, commander of the Military Air Transport Service (MATS), piloted the first Stratolifter from the factory to McGuire Air Force Base where it was assigned to his command's global airlift force.

By September, 1962, the last aircraft called for in the Boeing contract was delivered. By the end of September it was ready for its global airlift baptism.

The next 30 days in the life of this Stratolifter, identified only as MATS "Jet 4139," were tense, for October was to become a month of crisis.

For 4139, these Indian summer days were to be filled with African sun, Cuban rain, heat, cold, limitless stretches of blue sky, cargo, maintenance, humming engines, starry nights, countless people, and exotic places.

As so often happens during periods of crisis, the month began in routine fashion.

Capt. David W. Coville, a 40th Air Transport Squadron aircraft commander, was at the controls as the Stratolifter leaped off on its first October flight.

Heading a nine-man crew, Captain Coville darted from McGuire to Germany, and back to McGuire on October 3. Mission for the trip was airlifting Department of Defense cargo eastbound; precious cargo westbound.

Returning to the U.S., 4139 airlifted sick and injured American servicemen, bringing them home to hospitals and medical care aboard one of many aeromedical evacuation flights flown daily by MATS.

It took the streaking jet exactly 16 hours and 30 minutes to fly to Central Europe and back to this teeming MATS base in the New Jersey pinelands. Flying time for prop-driven aircraft on the same mission: 35 hours. The big jet had made the hop in less than half the time, with no en route stops.

The nine members of Captain Coville's crew were the first of 145 crew members to serve aboard 4139 during October.

The month would see 65 pilots, 30 navigators, 24 flight engineers, 21 load masters, four flight traffic specialists, and one aircraft mechanic assigned at various times to flight duties aboard the huge airlifter.

The reason for using so many crew members was explained by Maj. Gen. William P. Fisher, commander of the Eastern Transport Air Force (EASTAF), Atlantic arm of MATS:

"MATS cannot afford to assign one aircraft to one aircrew. We must keep our aircraft flying almost constantly, and manned always by well-rested crew members.

"When one of our aircrews completes a mission, a fresh aircrew takes its place and the aircraft keeps moving.

"In addition, we cannot assign a crew member to a single aircrew. Our crew members are assigned to transport squadrons and are scheduled for flights as needed.

"In MATS, our crew members average almost 100 hours' flying time per month, so you can see they're needed often!"

Lending emphasis to General Fisher's remarks is the fact that only one man made as many as three flights aboard 4139 during October, although nineteen others made at least two.

As the month sped by, 4139 rolled up 189 hours and 5 minutes' flying time.

Its pilots landed the sleek, silvery bird in Germany, Turkey, Greenland, Sweden, Congo, Libya, Cuba, and India and at bases in California and Florida.

Its navigators guided it over the Atlantic Ocean and the Mediterranean, Caribbean, and North Seas, and over a total of 31 countries.

It streaked along airways and great circle routes to span 101,115 miles of ocean, ice, desert, mountains, and plains.

It aided United Nations peace efforts in the Congo, and United States peace efforts in Cuba. And as its 30-day baptismal period came to an end, 4139 screamed aloft for India, bearing arms to Nehru for use against Chinese Communist aggressors.

Behind the spectacular flights of the great airlifter and the glamor of its ports of call was an enormous effort by hundreds of Air Force men and civilians; men who don't fly, but whose efforts keep our aircrews and aircraft flying.

These were men who serviced 4139 with jet fuel, who changed its tires, who loaded it with cargo, who checked its radios and radar, who washed it and swept it. These were mechanics, traffic specialists, flight followers, and supervisors who tied their many efforts into one great, hard-hitting effort.

Col. John B. Wallace, commander of the 1611th Air Transport Wing – the EASTAF unit which flies the Stratolifter – explains how these people work together so that his aircrews can fly the MATS global airlift mission.

"MATS Jet 4139 is assigned to our 1612th Organizational Maintenance Squadron for maintenance purposes. Working under our Maintenance Workload Control Center, this unit performs inspections, maintenance work, servicing, etc., and keeps the aircraft ready for flight.

"The squadron accomplishes post-flight and periodic inspections, and calls on our Field Maintenance and Communications and Electronics Maintenance squadrons for specialists.

"As the 1612th prepares the aircraft for flight, Workload Control schedules it for a programmed or special mission. Once scheduled, our Airlift Command Post (ACP) begins monitoring it.

"The ACP sees that it departs on schedule, with proper flight plan, fuel, and cabin load, and three hours before takeoff time, its flight crew is alerted and briefed so that it can safely fly its mission, whether to Calcutta, to Frankfurt, or wherever."

The aircraft was so new in October that by the end of the month it still had not undergone a periodic inspection – the fine-toothcombing conducted by MATS maintenance men each time a MATS aircraft piles up 400 hours' flying time.

Lt. Col. C. R. Greene, 1612th OMS commander, said that 4139 required absolutely no major maintenance during its 30-day baptismal.

Figures released by SSgt. Joe McCully of the 1611th's Analysis, Records, and Reports Division show the aircraft required 1,775 maintenance man-hours during the month.

These figures showed 495 hours for alert and servicing, 646 hours for nonscheduled maintenance, 514 hours for post-flight maintenance, and 119 hours for preflight maintenance.

Typical write-ups entered in the aircraft's records showed that a hydraulic line to the number four engine had to be replaced on October 5, and again on October 22, and a fuel feed line to the number four engine was installed on October 17.

According to CMSgt. W. H. Brown, 1612th line chief, these were among the most serious maintenance requirements encountered by 4139 in October.

Sergeant Brown said the great aircraft burned 403,522 gallons of JP-4 fuel and consumed nine gallons of oil during this month. He said it was moved and towed about the McGuire ramp eighteen times.

As 4139 whistled through these 30 crisis-laden days, it airlifted 19.3 million ton-miles of cargo and 41.2 million passenger-miles. Its powerful gear broke away from and was later mated to the earth for 74 takeoffs and landings.

If it had possessed ears, it would have heard a chorus of exotic sounds.

Near the middle of the 30-day period, its fuselage echoed the voices of Swedish soldiers returning to Stockholm from United Nations duty in the Congo. And toward the end of the period it reflected the grim silence of tough United States Marines flying into Guantanamo Naval Air Station, Cuba.

Returning from Germany on October 3, 4139 received a post-flight inspection from Sergeant Brown's maintenance men, and two days later – with Capt. George R. Mizell at the controls – it dashed to Spain, and on to Turkey. It returned to McGuire on October 6.

A WAF flight traffic specialist, A/3C Marsha L. Kennedy, was aboard 4139 for the Turkey turnaround. She was one of three women to serve aboard the aircraft during the 30-day period.

A severe change of climate came for 4139 on October 8, as an aircrew headed by Capt. Joseph C. Narlo took it to frigid Thule Air Base, Greenland, 800 miles from the North Pole.

Back to McGuire on October 9, the aircraft again received the attention of the 1611th's maintenance experts. They were preparing it for five days away from home — an everyday occurrence for prop-driven MATS aircraft, but an unusual event for a MATS Stratolifter.

It was about to become one of the first MATS jets ever employed in the two-year-old mission of supporting the United Nations in the Congo.

The next day the swept-back wings of 4139 cut the air as it raced above the North Atlantic for 7 hours and 50 minutes, hurtling non-stop from McGuire to Stockholm.

A day later, Congolese voices echoed about its four mighty Pratt & Whitney TF33-P-5 turbofan engines as it stopped briefly in Léopoldville, far to the south of the Equator. It had brought fresh Swedish troops to the Congo, and would return others to their Scandinavian homeland the same day.

On October 13 the big jet stopped at Wheelus Air Base, Libya, while headed for another Léopoldville turnaround. Its 18th Air Transport Squadron aircrew, headed by Maj. Keith D. Ricks, watched one of its sister ships take off from Léo that day for a record-breaking nonstop flight directly back to McGuire.

The next day 4139 came home via a "fireball" stop in Stockholm. To MATS aircrews, a "fireball" stop is one that lasts no more than two hours.

McGuire's maintenance men now took a real good look at their bird and found it well enough to send streaking back to Thule on October 19.

Two days later 4139 dashed to a stateside Marine base and within a few hours was setting down through a light rain shower at Guantanamo. Capt. James W. Haight was at the controls, and First Lt. Raymond L. Vannaman was the navigator.

Lieutenant Vannaman was the one crew member who logged three trips aboard the aircraft during the thirty-day period.

On October 23, 24, and 25, 4139 repeatedly circled and landed at McGuire as it compiled 32 hours and 10 minutes of local flying training. Instructor Pilot Capt. John W. Hand was in charge of two, five-hour periods, drilling other pilots on safe procedures, the foremost requirement in MATS flying.

On October 28 a well-known name in MATS was entered in the aircraft's records as the big bird made several stops in Florida, performing Cuban crisis missions.

That name belonged to Lt. Col. Vernon W. Hamann, a MATS

pilot who earlier that year broke a flock of existing world airlift records while at the controls of another MATS Stratolifter.

As the month ended, 4139 came home once again to the welcoming hands of Colonel Greene's maintenance men. This time they again geared it for a long haul: the airlift of arms from Germany to India.

As this hectic month came to a close, the great airlifter had returned to McGuire, the Indian airlift complete. Its 30-day baptismal – glorious, glamorous, and spectacular – was complete.

Its future may not have such a Hollywoodish aura as did this dramatic inaugural month, but sound McGuire MATS men like Sgt. W. H. Brown, Lt. Raymond L. Vannaman, Capt. John W. Hand, Maj. Keith D. Ricks, Lt. Col. C. R. Greene, and Col. John B. Wallace mean to see that its future is safe and sound; that it stands ready for global airlift anytime, anywhere, anyplace.

APPENDIX C

Chronology of Major MATS' Airlifts

THE Military Air Transport Service, organized June 1, 1948, was barely three weeks old as a major Air Force command when it was put to the test on the historic Berlin Airlift. Since that gigantic aerial movement of food, fuel, and other necessities of life, MATS has performed dozens of humanitarian airlifts and thousands of missions supporting emergency military actions, special exercises, and national policy. More so than other commands, MATS is responsive to breaking news events. At the same time, MATS meets the continuing routine airlift demands of the U.S. military forces around the world. This chronology includes only the more important airlifts, those of particular historic significance. Omitted are most of the recurring exercises with the Army as part of war-readiness training, and most one-time special lifts of such items as blood, antitoxins, medicines, and the MATS regularly scheduled, daily flights across the Atlantic and the Pacific and around the world.

Humanitarian Airlifts

1. BERLIN AIRLIFT (1948–49) – MATS helped supply Berlin with necessities of life, by air alone, for 15 months – airlifting almost 2½ million tons of food and fuel.

2. POLIO (1950) – Airlift of polio patients and of equipment to polio epidemic areas, both domestic and overseas, is a continuing activity in MATS. In January, 1953, a Citation of Honor was presented to MATS by the National Foundation for Infantile Paralysis. It recognized MATS' cooperation during the preceding two years in "transferring polio patients for treatment and in flying essential equipment into epidemic areas during emergencies."

3. INDIA (1950) – An earthquake in New Delhi brought MATS aircraft into Dum-Dum Airport, Calcutta, with emergency medical supplies.

4. MAGIC CARPET (1952) – Flying 75 missions in four days, 13 MATS aircraft airlifted 4,000 stranded Moslem pilgrims from Beirut, Lebanon, to Jidda, Saudi Arabia, nearest airport to their holy city of Mecca.

5. WAKE ISLAND (1952) – When Typhoon Olive struck the island, MATS aircraft flew in fresh water, food, medicine, cots, and blankets, and helped evacuate more than 450 people to Hawaii and Guam.

6. HUMANITY (1953) – Disastrous floods in Holland brought MATS in with food and other supplies for the stricken population, and sandbags to reinforce the sagging dikes.

7. WOUNDED WARRIOR (1954) – MATS evacuated 500 French troops, wounded in Indochina in the battle of Dien Bien Phu, from Japan to the United States, and then to France.

8. POLIO (March, 1956) – MATS airlifted iron lungs and other medical equipment to Buenos Aires, Argentina, during a polio epidemic.

9. SAFE HAVEN (1956–57) – MATS airlifted 14,263 Hungarian refugees, victims of Communist tyranny, from Germany to the United States.

10. JAPAN (September, 1959) – When the city of Nagoya was ravaged by Typhoon Vera, MATS C-124's shuttled more than 200 tons of food, clothing, blankets, and medical supplies from Tachikawa to Komaki Air Base.

11. MOROCCO (1960) – MATS airlifted 371,000 pounds of emergency equipment – shelters, cots and bedding – to Agadir, Morocco, and brought refugees out after earthquakes had buried the city.

12. BRAZIL (April, 1960) – When the Ceará and Tiauim areas of Brazil were devastated by floods, MATS C-124's airlifted emergency equipment, medical supplies, and two helicopters to the scene.

13. AMIGOS AIRLIFT (May-June, 1960) – MATS flew 77 mercy missions to Chile when earthquakes literally remade parts of that country. Homeless millions were aided by 877 tons of clothing, food, helicopters, and medical supplies, including two complete Army field hospitals. The longest airlift MATS had flown to that time, Amigos' average flying time one way was 25 hours to cover 4,500 miles.

14. POLIO (August, 1960) – MATS airlifted iron lungs to Japan, where more than 600 polio cases were reported on Hokkaido, northernmost island. The lungs were donated by the National Foundation.

15. EGYPT (August, 1961) – When an invasion of Army worms threatened Egypt's two-million-bale cotton crop, ten MATS aircraft airlifted nearly 240,000 pounds of a new American insecticide to Cairo.

16. TANGANYIKA (May, 1962) – Two MATS C-124 aircraft airdropped 1,543 tons of corn to 55,000 inhabitants of the Ruiji River Delta area near Dar es Salaam, Tanganyika, when floods cut off overland supply routes. During a 30-day period, the aircraft made 77 flights, dropping 20 tons per mission.

17. PROJECT IDA (October-November, 1962) – MATS C-124 Globemasters and C-133 Cargomasters airlifted 444 tons of relief supplies to the earthquake-torn people of Tehran, Iran. Included in this 3,275-mile airlift from Germany across the Middle East to the Iranian capital was one complete field hospital.

18. GUAM – TYPHOON KAREN (November, 1962) – Devastating 175-mph winds of Typhoon Karen had barely subsided when the first of 50 MATS jet and prop-driven aircraft began landing on the rain-soaked runways of Anderson Air Force Base, Guam,

with relief supplies and equipment. MATS airlifted more than 970 tons of material — from huge electric generators to blankets and clothing. Returning aircraft evacuated more than 760 dependents and servicemen whose homes had been shattered by the island's most severe storm in recorded history.

19. ICE ISLAND-ARLIS II (November, 1962) — Ten scientists camped for the Arctic winter on a 1½- by 3-mile ice floe known as Arlis II, floating 300 miles from the North Pole, radioed an urgent appeal for fuel. Two MATS C-124 Globemasters, operating from Elmendorf Air Force Base, Alaska, 1,800 miles from the scientists, air-dropped 78 tons of fuel to the men in 15 round-trip, 17-hour missions. The drop target was only a tiny flare-marked "T" flickering in the Arctic night in minus 30-degree temperatures on the ice below.

Global Airlifts

1. BLUE JAY (1951) — MATS flew heavy construction equipment, builders, housing, and supplies to Greenland for the key base at Thule, advancing the completion date by a full year.

2. KOREA (1953) — During the Korean action, June, 1950-July, 1953, MATS airlifted nearly 50,000 combat casualties and patients to the United States.

3. SUEZ (1956) — MATS airlifted 1,300 Colombian and Indian troops from Bogotá and Agra to the United Nations staging area in Naples, Italy, to supplement the UN police force in the Suez area.

4. DEEP FREEZE (October, 1957, to 1963) — In December, 1962, MATS Douglas C-124 Globemasters ended six years of seasonal flying as members of the Air Force-Navy team resupplying scientific stations in the Antarctic. During that time the aircraft, operated by the 63rd Troop Carrier Wing stationed at Donaldson Air Force Base, South Carolina, air-dropped about 4,000 tons of supplies from the main Antarctic base at McMurdo Sound to remote stations near and at the South Pole. Beginning in 1963, Lockheed C-130E Hercules, newer, faster, and longer range,

picked up the MATS portion of the mission. The performance of the C-124's in the Antarctic cold strengthened the concept of airlift flexibility by doing in a few weeks (each year) a job that would have taken surface transportation several months. During Deep Freeze III, a C-124 air-dropped a seven-ton tractor to an isolated site, and during Deep Freeze 62 (October-December, 1961), three C-124's made the longest flight in Antarctic history, a 3,100-mile round trip to airdrop supplies. Also during Deep Freeze 62, Lt. Gen. Joe W. Kelly became the first MATS commander to visit the operation. MATS vice commander, Maj. Gen. Raymond J. Reeves, visited Deep Freeze 63.

5. LEBANON (1958) – MATS airlifted 5,500 tons of cargo and 5,400 troops to the Middle East in support of the Lebanese government, also supporting the move of a TAC Composite Air Strike Force to the area.

6. TAIWAN (1958) – MATS flew 144 airlift trips to the Far East when the crisis arose in the Formosan Straits, supporting the move of a Composite Air Strike Force, and airlifting a squadron of F-104 Starfighters to Taiwan.

7. HARDTACK (1958) – MATS airlifted more than 14,000 tons of cargo and 13,000 personnel, as well as providing 1,100 of its own technical personnel, in support of the nuclear bomb tests at the Eniwetok Proving Ground.

8. THOR LIFT (1958) – MATS airlifted Thor IRBM's and their equipment from California to England, flying a record 80 trips in November.

9. FIRST ATLAS AIRLIFT (1959) – On November 3, a MATS C-133 Cargomaster airlifted, for the first time, an Atlas intercontinental ballistic missile – from Miramar Naval Air Station, San Diego, to ARDC's Ballistic Missile Division at Francis E. Warren Air Force Base, Wyoming.

10. BIG SLAM (1960) – MATS almost doubled its aircraft flying rate during March in a test of its ability to surge to a wartime pace. As part of this exercise, it joined with the Army in the

largest peacetime airlift exercise in military history (Big Slam Puerto Pine), airlifting 21,095 troops and 10,925 tons of their combat equipment from the U.S. to Puerto Rico and back.

11. CONGO AIRLIFT (1960–63) – MATS C-124 Globemasters and C-118 Liftmasters (and in November, 1962, pure-jet C-135 Stratolifters) by the end of November had chalked up more than 2,000 missions in history's longest airlift – reaching 5,000 miles from Europe around Africa's coast to Léopoldville in the Congo. MATS entered the United Nations airlift under direction of the United States Air Forces in Europe (USAFE) 322nd Air Division, July 16, 1960, and at the peak had 60 aircraft committed. By the end of 1962, about 49,000 troops and 11,000 tons of cargo had been airlifted to and from points as far away as New Delhi, India.

12. LONG PASS (1961) and GREAT SHELF (1962) – In February, 1961, MATS participated in Long Pass, the first strategic deployment airlift exercise of its size to the Pacific. It used 132 aircraft to move a battle group of the Strategic Army Corps (STRAC) and equipment for a Tactical Air Command Composite Strike Force (CASF) to Clark Air Base, the Philippines, and back again. In February, 1962, MATS used 120 airlift aircraft of all types in a similar exercise, Great Shelf, to the same area. This time it moved 2,300 Army paratroops of STRAC and 1,100 tons of their equipment over the 7,600-statute-mile route.

13. EXERCISE CHECKMATE II (September, 1961) – More than 100 MATS global airlift aircraft from EASTAF and WESTAF participated in this fall exercise from the United States to Turkey. They airlifted about 2,000 Army troops from the 101st Airborne Division at Fort Campbell, Kentucky, and about 900 tons of their equipment on the 12,000-mile round trip. During the exercise, about 300 MATS airmen and officers lived in tents for about three weeks handling maintenance and communications. Lt. Gen. Joe W. Kelly, MATS commander, was on hand to greet the first arriving aircraft. Despite "miserable" weather, no accidents or incidents occurred.

14. EXERCISE LONG THRUST II (January, 1962) – MATS'

new four-engined jets, the Boeing C-135 Stratolifter, made their first appearance in a major airlift when 12 of them airlifted nearly 800 Army troops over the Arctic Circle from Fort Lewis, Washington, to central Germany. They made the nonstop trip in little more than 10 hours compared to the piston-engined aircraft which averaged between 30 and 35 hours along normal routes. Altogether, more than 100 MATS aircraft moved 5,300 troops of three battle groups of the Army's 4th Infantry Division in the deployment phase. The jets brought one battle group back. In Germany, the troops participated in ground maneuvers with NATO forces.

Since that first Long Thrust exercise (Long Thrust I was canceled), several troop rotations to Germany have been held, using the jets only. These each have operated under the Long Thrust designation. In July, Long Thrust IV set a new record by airlifting one battle group from Forbes Air Force Base, Kansas, to Germany, and another back to Seattle, Washington, all within a total of 45 hours.

15. STAIR STEP (1961) and HIGH TOP (1962) – When the Reserve Forces were called to active duty in October, 1961, MATS airlift force and technical units provided support for their movement to Europe. Operation Stair Step was the name given to the deployment of Air National Guard fighter units overseas, and Operation High Top was the redeployment, June-August, 1962. In High Top, for example, more than 260 missions were flown by MATS aircraft of all types, including the C-97's which themselves had been called to active duty. These aircraft returned more than 9,600 ANG personnel and 1,400 tons of equipment.

16. SOUTHERN EXPRESS (October, 1962) – During this NATO exercise in Europe, MATS airlifted NATO troops from bases in Central Europe to Greece and back. Between October 7 and 13, MATS C-124 Globemasters and C-118 Liftmasters flew about 250 missions to move 3,000 troops and more than 470 tons of cargo to the exercise area and return.

17. ROTAPLAN (October 15-21, 1962) – A series of planned rotations of Army troops between U.S. and European bases calls for large airlifts in a short time. MATS jets and propeller aircraft

accomplished the first Rotaplan in October, 1962, airlifting a total of 3,513 troops and 27 tons of cargo in seven days.

18. CUBAN CRISIS (October, 1962) — In the midst of one of the heaviest airlift schedules it has ever had (more than 17 airlifts under way or developing during October and November), MATS was called on to support the buildup of forces in the southeastern part of the United States. On October 16, MATS began working at its wartime activity rate. Between October 16 and the end of the month, MATS airlifted thousands of troops and thousands of tons in hundreds of sorties from bases throughout the country into Florida and Guantanamo Bay, Cuba. Included in this was the first major airlift of Marines and their combat gear by MATS. Also, during this buildup, MATS lost its first C-135 Stratolifter jet while it was engaged in an ammunition airlift to Guantanamo Bay. All three of the technical services stepped up activities to provide close weather, rescue, and documentation support to the buildup.

19. INDIAN AIRLIFT (November 2-10, 1962) — MATS, still involved in missions connected with the Cuban crisis, was called on to react to a call for arms to India to stem the Communist Chinese invasion. The airlift required the movement of 980 tons of small arms more than 6,000 miles from Rhein-Main, Germany, to Dum-Dum Airport, Calcutta. This "no notice" airlift was accomplished in eight days by MATS C-135 Stratolifter jets.

20. BIG LIFT (October 22-24, 1963) — In the first time that a full Army division and elements of a Tactical Air Command Strike Force were ferried across the ocean in one big airlift, 15,358 officers and men of the 2nd Armored Division, their support troops, and 504 tons of battle equipment were airlifted by 204 MATS aircraft from eight bases in the South and southwestern U.S. (namely Texas) to France and Germany. They were accompanied by 116 tactical fighters and reconnaissance aircraft of the Composite Air Strike Force (CASF) who flew across the Atlantic "under their own steam." The entire operation was accomplished in 2½ days, employing 234 missions. The C-135 Stratolifter jets made the 5,600-mile trip in 10½ hours nonstop, carrying 75 troops each. It took the C-124 Globemasters three

times as long, with refueling stops at Bermuda and the Azores, to carry 80 troops and cargo. Following NATO ground maneuvers in Europe, the troops were lifted back to the United States on November 21, 1963.

21. QUICK RELEASE (January 30, 1964) — MATS airlifted the troops of the 25th Infantry Division from their base in Hawaii, across the Pacific, to Okinawa.

Index